HOW WOULD YOU ANSWER THIS LETTER
IF YOU WERE ANN LANDERS?

"Our 20-year-old son returned home from college for Easter vacation. He said, 'Mom and Dad, I hope you will be objective about this. I've got a date tonight. The girl is a sure thing. I know I can score. May I use my bedroom or are you going to force me to use my car?'"

AND MUCH MORE
IN

ANN LANDERS'
TRUTH IS STRANGER . . .

ANN LANDERS SAYS
TRUTH IS STRANGER...

by Ann Landers

BANTAM BOOKS
TORONTO · NEW YORK · LONDON
A NATIONAL GENERAL COMPANY

ANN LANDERS SAYS:
TRUTH IS STRANGER . . .
*A Bantam Book / published by arrangement with
Prentice-Hall, Inc.*

PRINTING HISTORY
Prentice-Hall edition published November 1968
Bantam edition published January 1970

Bantam Books are published by Bantam Books, Inc., a National
General company. Its trade-mark, consisting of the words "Bantam
Books" and the portrayal of a bantam, is registered in the United
States Patent Office and in other countries. Marca Registrada.
Bantam Books, Inc., 666 Fifth Avenue, New York, N.Y. 10019.

PRINTED IN THE UNITED STATES OF AMERICA

For Jules
Who continues to do the impossible . . . he
keeps two women happy—
Ann Landers and Eppie Lederer

ACKNOWLEDGMENTS

No writer, living or dead, ever leaned more heavily on the counsel and benevolence of others. I have been blessed with a spectacular assortment of brainy friends who have provided me with vital information on a moment's notice. The list of those who have given so generously of their time and knowledge is a long one. I am reluctant, for the sin of omission is a grave one, but I shall attempt to thank those to whom I feel most deeply indebted.

My eternal gratitude to John G. Trezevant, Executive Vice-President of the Chicago *Sun-Times* and the Chicago *Daily News*. This cherished friend continues to edit my column although in August of 1966 he was transplanted from the editorial side of the *Sun-Times* to the thick-carpeted, walnut-paneled executive offices.

My principal medical consultant is Dr. Robert Stolar, Clinical Associate Professor of Medicine, Georgetown University, Washington, D. C. Dr. Stolar has earned the Golden Ear Award for listening to this book, one chapter at a time, over the long-distance telephone.

Special thanks to Dr. John P. Merrill for his guidance and counsel. Dr. Merrill is Chief of the Cardio-Renal Department, Peter Bent Brigham Hospital, Boston, and Associate Professor of Medicine at Harvard Medical School.

My principal psychiatric consultants are Dr. Zigmond Lebensohn, Chief of Psychiatry, Sibley Memorial Hospital, Washington, D. C.; Dr. Edwin M. Litin, Chief of Psychiatry at Mayo Clinic, Rochester, Minnesota; Dr. Phillip Solomon, Clinical Professor of Psychiatry at Harvard, and Dr. William Simpson, Director of the Menninger School of Psychiatry, Topeka, Kansas. These distinguished gentlemen have served me faithfully and well.

I would like to express my appreciation to Lowell Sachnoff of Chicago for providing me with answers to legal problems, and to Jack Pritzker, another Chicago attorney, for serving as my consultant on divorce law for ten years. In 1966 Jack sent me a divorce manual and suggested I do it myself.

I am grateful to Harold Anderson, my former Syndicate Chief and to Robert Hall, President of Publishers-Hall Syndicate. Those two gentlemen have made this column available to millions of readers all over the world.

To Elizabeth Carr of Publishers-Hall Syndicate a warm caress for handling the mechanics of my copy and catching the bloopers that escaped all other eyes.

A low bow to Dr. Maynard Cook, Chicago, for serving as my consultant on dentistry.

A special encomium for my experts on religion, Dr. Jacob Weinstein, Rabbi Emeritus of Temple K.A.M. Chicago; Dr. Dow Kirkpatrick, Pastor of the First Methodist Church, Evanston, Illinois; Rev. Theodore Hesburgh, President of the University of Notre Dame, and Monsignor John J. Paul, La Crosse, Wisconsin.

My affectionate thanks to Bailey K. Howard, President of Field Enterprises; Emmett Dedmon, Editor of the Chicago *Sun-Times;* James Hoge, Executive Editor, and Ralph Otwell, Managing Editor, for making me feel that I am a member of this remarkable newspaper family.

My acknowledgments would be shamefully incomplete if I failed to express my gratitude to Wilbur Munnecke, now in semiretirement at Leland, Michigan, and Larry Fanning, Publisher of the Anchorage, Alaska, *Daily News*. Will "discovered" Ann Landers in 1955 and Larry edited her copy for ten years.

My special gratitude to spartan Valerie Topaz, my principal assistant, who carried a heavy burden while I was gathering material for this book.

To Norma Born, a halo and a set of angel wings for typing the manuscript and offering invaluable suggestions.

My warm thanks to Paul Hirt, Director of Promotion, Chicago *Sun-Times* and *Daily News*, and Richard Sherry, Promotion Chief of Publishers-Hall, for their superb cooperation, over and above the call of duty.

A pat on two smart heads—one for Mrs. Newton Minow for naming the last chapter and another to daughter Margo Coleman for naming the book. The title I wanted to use was, "My Mailman Has a Hernia" —but my mailman wouldn't let me.

Contents

ANN LANDERS SAYS:
TRUTH IS STRANGER . . .

One

CONFESSIONS OF ANN LANDERS

My mailman has a hernia. And it's not surprising. Every day the poor fellow brings me approximately one thousand letters, plus a gaggle of magazines, the *Wall Street Journal*, and *The New York Times*.

My heart goes out to my mailman, but I can no more lighten his burden than I can ease my own. We are both trapped. So long as my syndicated column appears in print, there will be a steady deluge of mail. The mailman will have to lug it and I will read it.

If this sounds like a subtle bid for sympathy, don't fall for it. I am firmly convinced that the majority of gripers need something to gripe about. It provides them with an opportunity to unleash negativism. And Yours Truly is no exception. If I didn't love this work I would have abandoned it long ago.

After writing the Ann Landers column for thirteen years I can truthfully say that I still anticipate each day with enthusiasm. I approach each bundle of letters with a fresh and exquisite curiosity. Writing a daily advice column is fascinating. It is challenging. Rewarding. My readers stimulate me, insult me, love me, provoke me, and clobber me when I am wrong. But I take my lumps and like it. My column has me hopelessly hooked. If there were anything in this world I'd rather do, I'd be doing it—or at least trying.

Who writes to Ann Landers anyway? It could be

1

anyone, and there are days when I'm sure it is *every-*
one. My readers are unpredictable, supersensitive,
warmhearted, irascible, sharp-eyed, sharp-tongued,
fiercely critical, and beautifully loyal. They may well
be the lovingest, hatingest, writingest cross section of
humanity in all the world, and I confess I love them
dearly.

Before I became Ann Landers, I was under the
impression that only a nut would write to a newspaper
columnist for help with a personal problem. But I was
wrong. I hear from every conceivable segment of society. The people who write to Ann Landers are from 6
years of age to 101 years of age. They live on subur-
ban estates and in the city's slums. They are extremely
intelligent and pathetically ignorant. Some of the letters I receive are difficult to read. The spelling is poor
and the handwriting virtually illegible. Somehow one
expects this. The real surprise is the number of letters
from the so-called cream of society. These double-
dome correspondents rarely ask for advice; they are
"only seeking an opinion." Or they write to unload.
"If I don't get this off my chest I'll blow my top!" "I
can't talk to anyone in town about this problem. We
are a prominent family and I just couldn't take the hu-
miliation." "I'm not writing for advice, Ann, I know
what I must do. I want to put it all down on paper and
see if it makes sense. I may not even mail it."

Almost half of my mail comes from men. Surprised?
I was, considering that a great many men hide my column under the sports page. And what do these men
write to Ann Landers about? You name it and I've
heard it. They want to know if they should run for office, marry for money, wear a toupee, change sexes,
burn their draft cards, enter a monastery, smoke marihuana, marry a stepsister, leave their bodies to a medical school. One man wrote to ask if his wife had a

right to insist that he wear a bicycle horn strapped to his head at night to wake him up when he snores.

I have come to expect the unexpected. Every batch of mail contains a surprise, an explosive reaction, a bitter invective, and a warmly worded compliment. There's always a laugh and you can be sure there are heartbreakers, too. I learned early, however, to take my work seriously but not to let it get me. And this, my friends, is not easy when I encounter a problem that, but for the grace of God, could have been my own.

I've been told to drop dead, get lost, stop playing God, and quit making up crazy letters. I've been called a crummy broad, a square from Iowa, and a broken-down museum piece. The cocktail set insists I am a reformed drunk who is determined to dry up the world. I've been accused of being a public relations agent for the American Medical Association and a mouthpiece for the American Psychiatric Association. (With amazing regularity I am asked, "How can you, in good conscience, tell people to go to a psychiatrist when most psychiatrists are nutty as hell?")

My work is immensely satisfying but it is also enormously demanding. Every letter that has a name and address gets a personal reply in the mail. Although I have eleven assistants, I put in ten or twelve hours every day. When I go on lecture trips my column must be prepared in advance. Every word that appears under my byline is written by me. To maintain quality 365 days a year is difficult, and there are no honest shortcuts.

It is obvious that giving advice is an awesome responsibility, and I accept this responsibility with the seriousness it deserves. The Ann Landers column now appears in over seven hundred papers from Anchorage to Johannesburg. From Portland, Maine, to Tokyo. The readership of the column is estimated at 54 million. This is the largest reading audience in the world. Staggering? Yes. Frightening? No. I view it as a challenge and a unique opportunity to shine a spotlight on ignorance and fear and stupidity.

I do not attempt to substitute for the clergyman, the physician or the analyst, the lawyer or the social worker. In fact, I urge thousands of people every day to get professional help. I have a complete file of the service agencies for every city in which my column appears, indicating precisely what facilities are available in each of the seven-hundred-plus cities.

Since I am not an expert on any particular subject, I lean heavily on those who are. I spend hours on the telephone every day, probing, learning, gathering for my readers the best answers from those who are best qualified to give them. These specialists are my friends —top authorities in the fields of medicine, psychiatry, religion, law, business, politics, welfare, and education. They may be thousands of miles away but they are as close as my telephone. The advice I give to the shoe clerk in Toronto, the student in Mexico City, or the housewife in Chicago may be free to *them,* but at the end of the month my telephone bill looks like the defense budget.

I do not deceive myself that I can solve problems. Each indivdual must solve his own. And I know, too, that some problems are insoluble; the best one can do is learn to live with them.

My primary purpose is to serve as a catalyst—an unbiased observer—to offer an ear, or a shoulder to cry on. As one reader put it, "If anyone had told me I would end up writing to an agony column for help, I would have said they were crazy, but I need someone who will listen and there isn't anybody else."

My column has given me a unique opportunity to view human behavior at its worst and at its best. It is a daily chronicle of man's inhumanity to man, an authentic testimony to the quiet heroism of the folks next door. It is the ugliness and self-destruction, the beauty, the sacrifice, the agony and the ecstasy of Mary and John Doe. And they tell it like it is.

And how is it? It is armies of ordinary citizens who drag their headaches and their ulcers to work every day. It is the most gigantic fake-out of all time. These millions of actors deserve an Academy Award for just getting out of bed in the morning.

The success of the Ann Landers column underscores for me, at least, the central tragedy of our society—the loneliness, the insecurity, the fear that bedevils, cripples, and paralyzes so many of us. The column presents daily evidence that financial success and social and political status open no doors to peace of mind and contentment.

This book was not my idea. It was yours. For the past thirteen years I have received thousands of letters saying, "It's a nuisance to clip and paste columns. Often I lose them or they get too ratty to put in the scrapbook. Why don't you, Ann Landers, put your best columns between hard covers?" So I did.

—Ann Landers

Two

SEX IN MARRIAGE

Sex is like dynamite. What you use it for makes all the difference in the world. Sex can be a challenge, an ego-booster, a weapon, a duty, an obsession, a bore, a trauma, a pastime, a tranquilizer, an insult, or a contact sport. It can be the most meaningful, elevating, and exhilarating of all human experiences—and it can be the emptiest.

Women complain about sex more often than men. Their gripes fall into two major categories: 1) Not enough, 2) Too much. While a wife from Topeka writes, "My husband is a nut. He keeps asking me why we can't have a happy, normal marriage and forget about sex?" another wife from El Paso moans, "My husband has the bedroom manners of an elk. He is after me morning, noon, and night. Any animal can have a sex life. What I want is a *love* life."

My mail reflects an alarming degree of ambivalence, hypocrisy, and just plain ignorance on the subject. The frustrated and unfulfilled who write about sex problems are from thirteen to eighty. They are teeny-boppers, bus drivers, bank presidents, Boston Back Bay matrons, students, professors, waitresses—single, married, divorced, and widowed. Some of the letters are unbearably poignant. Others are filled with four-letter words.

Superior intelligence and mental acuity do not insure a successful sex life. Many financial and professional giants are inadequate or nonfunctional bed-partners, and their marriages fall apart because of it. Some semiliterate clods, on the other hand, enjoy sex immensely. Why? Because it is not what we *know* about sex, but how we *feel* about it that counts.

More divorces start in the bedroom than in any other room of the house. And this is only part of the story. Millions of married couples who appear to be compatible have unsatisfactory sex relations or none at all.

If a young woman has been reared to believe that sex is sinful, nasty, something that must be "put up with," she will not suddenly become a cooperative love-partner merely because a clergyman has made it legal. Girls who were warned from childhood to beware of men because "they are all after one thing," will find it difficult, if not impossible, to relax and enjoy it. Boys who were raised to believe that "nice girls don't do such things" often have difficulty achieving satisfactory sex relations with a wife. They can make it only with tramps or prostitutes because sex with a tarnished woman produces no guilt.

Women frequently ask, "How much sex is enough?" They then describe their anger and resentment toward a husband whose sexual demands leave them exhausted. When I publish such a letter, I receive dozens of replies from equally unhappy wives who write, "I wish I could trade husbands with Mrs. Dead Tired. My slob falls asleep in front of the TV every night with a beer can in his hand."

One of the questions most frequently asked (invariably by women) is, "What is considered moral between married couples?" I have consulted physicians and clergymen of all faiths on this subject and they concur that nothing is immoral, indecent, or undesirable in married love provided it is agreeable to both parties and there are no painful or harmful effects.

When couples have difficulty achieving satisfaction, I urge them to discuss it openly—without shame. If a wife finds certain aspects of lovemaking unrewarding or unpleasant, she should not suffer in martyred silence. The ability to keep the arteries of communication open on all subjects is the hallmark of a healthy marriage.

A husband should not be ashamed to suggest innovations, nor should a woman, for that matter. Sexual intercourse is the language of love. A man and his wife should have no qualms about expressing their love in any manner that is pleasing to them.

Each of us needs to be freed from the prison of our aloneness. The perfect sex experience does this—and more. It is a spiritual and emotional blending of Man and Woman. For those very special moments the universe belongs exclusively to them. No one else exists.

Perfect physical love is a gift not reserved for a privileged few—the wealthy or the wise or the young. It belongs to anyone who knows how to love and how to give.

———

The following letters are from readers who had trouble with sex, so they wrote to Ann Landers.

Dear Ann Landers: I'm not a cold person. I love my husband and I also like sex. Perhaps I should be honest and say I *used* to like sex. Since we moved closer to his place of business Bill has been coming home to lunch four and five days a week. Sometimes he doesn't even eat. Do you get the picture? I hope so, because I need your help. We have three children who need to be fed and bathed, plus the laundry and the cooking and the housework. I am much more relaxed in the evening and never say No. Am I wrong to refuse to make like Madame Pompadour at noon?—*Frantic Frances*

Dear Fran: No. Tell your husband you married him for better or for worse—but not for lunch.

Dear Ann Landers: I was deeply disappointed in your advice to Frantic Frances whose husband comes home for lunch. Should a husband be looked upon with scorn and contempt just because he is healthy and normal? An overwhelming majority of American wives are so involved with their tea parties, card playing, and country-club martini drinking that they are too darned pooped to satisfy the emotional needs of their husbands. No wonder the divorce rate is zooming. A smart wife should be thrilled that her husband *wants* to come home for lunch. You failed every red-blooded American male in your audience when you gave that lousy answer.—*Bitterly Disappointed Male*

Dear Bitterly: Apparently I disappointed a substantial number of red-blooded American Females, too. One woman wrote, "I wish my old man would appear for *dinner*. I never know where he is from one day to the next." A reader in Chattanooga moaned, "Does the guy live in Tennessee? If he does please send him to my house for lunch. I'm a good cook and I'd be happy to see him." As for Bitterly Disappointed, show me one tea-partying, card-playing, martini-swigging wife and I'll show you five hundred floor-scrubbing, shirt-ironing, diaper-folding women who are busy from dawn till dusk trying to take care of their families. It is absurd to suggest that a wife should be on 24-hour call like an inhalator squad—ready for romance at the drop of a hint.

Dear Ann Landers: Thanks for the advice you gave Frantic Frances. I traveled that same road for twenty years and finally divorced my sex maniac. I nearly had a nervous breakdown. No matter what I was doing, what my mood—happy, sad, sick, or well—my husband (who showed no hint of his carnal appetite before marriage) was breathing down my neck—leering, panting, pawing, until I couldn't stand the sight of him. "Night and Day" was written for him, but it meant only one thing. Sex. A knot on a tree reminded him of a woman's shape. Mentally he undressed every woman he saw, and he never failed to tell me in detail of his reactions. You will probably say he's sick, but so far as I know he is still running around loose. I've had enough sex to last me a lifetime. Now you can throw this letter away, but I feel better for having written it.—*Statue Of Liberty*

What a life! Feast or famine! There ain't no justice. Read on.

Dear Ann Landers: May I respond to the reader who wrote: "Show me a man, either single or married, sick, well, or dying, who would turn down sex, and I will happily eat the Sunday edition of *The Washington Post.*" I would like to say, "Start nibblin', dear heart." I married a man who has the sex drive of a dead battery. My sisters drew the same kind. You suggest that these "disinterested" males go to a doctor and find out what is wrong. A fine suggestion, but what if they won't go? Furthermore, I am 99 percent certain that the problem is not physical but mental. My "dead battery" is healthy as a horse. I can't recall the last time he had a headache. What about this, Ann Landers? Am I right or wrong?—*Baby It's Cold In The House*

Dear Baby: You are probably right. The vast majority of "disinterested" men have no organic problem. But it's always advisable to go to a physician and make sure. When no organic problem is present, a husband should accept the fact that he has an emotional problem. He owes it to his wife as well as to himself to see a therapist and get rid of the hornet in his helmet.

And now a male point of view:

Dear Ann Landers: I'm getting pretty sick of your pat answers. They are beginning to sound as if you crank them out of a machine. I refer specifically to your replies to husbands who complain about iceberg wives. My wife has been a stationary snowdrift from the day we married. For fourteen years I have put up with her excuses, and "duty" expressions of marital bliss. I first started to kid her about finding satisfaction elsewhere if she didn't warm up. Later I stopped kidding and made the threat in earnest. Her answer was, "I don't care what you do so long as you don't bother *me.*" I am thirty-five. My wife is thirty-three. This is too young to dry up and blow away. She is an excellent mother, a fine housekeeper, a gracious hostess, and active in the League of Women Voters, but she is more than cold—she's frozen. Be practical and give me an answer that does more than take up two inches of newspaper space.—*Starvation Diet*

Dear S.D.: Many are cold but few are frozen. Your wife is probably the product of a guilt-ridden, inhibited mother who believed all men were beasts because that's what her mother told her. You say your wife is an iceberg. This is an apt description in more ways than one. Four fifths of an iceberg are below the surface. Your job is to get acquainted with the whole woman. Your iceberg—I mean your wife—should talk to her doctor. She is not living up to her responsibilities to you. Furthermore, she is cheating herself. You should see a doctor, too. A French philosopher once said, "There are no cold women—only clumsy men."

Dear Ann Landers: I have been married for four years and have undergone the third degree at least one thousand times. My husband refuses to believe he is the only man who has ever made love to me. I raise my right hand, he was my first sweetheart. We started to go together when I was fifteen. I was nineteen when we were married. There has never been another man in my life and there never will be, unless my husband makes me so miserable with his accusations that I am forced to divorce him to keep my sanity. I'm thankful he doesn't accuse me in the presence of others. He waits until we are alone and the lights are out. It's always the same—"If you will just tell me, I promise I won't get mad. I'll never throw it up to you." Ann, it's almost as if he *wishes* there was somebody else. Why does he behave this way?—*Not Guilty*

Dear Not Guilty: Some people obtain sexual stimulation from fantasies. In fact, they cannot function without the help of these one-act plays. The thoughts they entertain (or the thoughts that entertain them) never cross their minds any other time. Your husband conjures up mental images of you with other men because it excites him. He knows very well it's all in his head, so don't let his questions bother you.

Dear Ann: During fifteen years of marriage I never glanced sideways—that is, until a new executive joined my husband's firm. He was handsome, sophisticated, and I fell like a ton of bricks. That look in his eye let me know he was reading me, and my answer was Yes. The way to "get acquainted," I strategized, was to invite him and his wife for dinner. She and I would become friends, and you know the rest. One look at his Mrs. chilled my ardor. They arrived late and she was plastered. Her conversation was incredibly banal and boring. He gave her long looks—which she ignored. Their relationship was obviously a horror. How could *he* have chosen *her?* The gentleman has never looked good to me since. So, perhaps it's not such a bad idea after all, girls. Get to know the man's wife.—*White Plains*

Dear White Plains: Here's another letter, same subject, different twist.

Dear Ann: After eighteen years of marriage, my wife confessed she was having an affair with—of all people—her best friend's husband. No, she didn't want a divorce. And neither did he. There were six children involved. Would I stand by until the fire burned itself out? I told her, "Yes, I'll try." The next day I telephoned the other man's wife and invited her to my office for a chat. She had known—instinct, she called it —and was pretending not to see. I admired her character and her courage. And I noticed for the first time how terribly attractive she was. We've been comforting each other ever since, and I hope my wife never gets tired of the other guy.—*Not Grieving*

Dear Ann Landers: I've been married to an almost perfect husband for thirteen years. We get along beautifully so long as he keeps his hands off me, but *this* he does not want to do. I married him thinking his good qualities and generosity would make up for the missing ingredient, but I was wrong. His kisses leave me cold. His lovemaking is clumsy. I get nothing from him. I thought he'd improve but he has gotten worse. Shall I divorce him, provided I can find grounds? Or should I stick with him for the children?—*No Pulse*

Dear No Pulse: You say you married this man for "his good qualities," but you don't say why *he* married *you*. One thing is certain: he didn't marry you to "keep his hands off." The unsatisfactory sexual aspect of your marriage is a reflection of your dissatisfaction with the whole man. You two need outside help. Divorce is not the answer. Cure it. Don't kill it.

Dear Ann Landers: A social craze called Mixed Mates has hit town. The invitation we received yesterday read: "You are cordially invited for cocktails and dinner at Bill and Mary X's home on January 25. But you can't come with your husband. He must escort someone else's wife. You will not know the identity of your escort until he arrives. Your husband will soon receive a phone call assigning a date. But it must be kept a deep, dark secret. Of course you will be taken home by the man who brought you. R.S.V.P." I don't want to be a wet firecracker, but the whole idea offends me. My husband says it's novel and should be fun. What would we tell our teen-age children about such a party? Help, please.—*Fraidy Cat*

Dear Fraidy: Tell your teen-age children that married people go to parties together and they come home together, which is why you and their father cannot accept this tasteless invitation.

Dear Ann Landers: This letter is no gag. I look like Paul Newman, and it is ruining my life. I'm thirty years old, happily married, and the father of three children. I'm a steady church-goer. The girl who runs the elevator in this building takes me down to the basement, pushes the stop button, and tries to get friendly. The baby-sitter keeps asking me to kiss her good night when I drive her home because I am so "mature" and she is sick of high-school boys. When I stop at a lunch counter, women come over and ask for my autograph. I tell them they are mistaken, but they sit down and want to get acquainted. Yesterday my wife saw me having a cup of coffee with a beautiful young girl from the office who has been making a pest of herself lately. I may be in a little trouble at home. Please give me some help.—*Case of Mistaken Identity*

Dear Case: Why don't you arm youself with a whip and a chair—or wear goggles and a fright wig? A thirty-year-old man who doesn't want to get mixed up with dames knows how to steer clear without any help from me, so put that show on the road, Dad.

Dear Ann Landers: So now I'm a prostitute—according to you. In a recent column you said, "When sex is used by a wife as payment for favors and is withheld as punishment, it places the marriage at the level of prostitution." What else can a woman do when sex is her only effective weapon? I've been married to this character for eighteen years, and it's the only approach that works. My husband's income exceeds $40,000 a year. Every woman I know gets an allowance but me. My husband doesn't believe a wife needs an allowance. He says, "What for? You're home all day." The only way I can get any money out of him is to nail him when he's in an amorous mood. Now, do you blame me?—*The Professional Amateur*

Dear Amateur: If this has been going on for eighteen years, you aren't going to change it. A bouquet of skunk cabbage to your husband for reducing you to such a level.

Dear Ann Landers: Is it adultery if a married man goes out once a week with a woman who is also married and whose husband works nights? My husband swears no sex is involved. According to him, adultery means sex between a married person and a single person. What is your verdict?—*Little Egypt*

Dear Little Egypt: Adultery is a sexual relationship between a married person and another person who is not his spouse. I suggest your husband knock off his weekly "sexless" date. If the woman's husband catches up with him, the guy is not likely to discuss definitions. He may just give him a clop in the chops.

Dear Ann Landers: Three years ago I wrote to you about my husband and another woman. When I learned of the affair, I was crushed. He swore the affair meant nothing and said if I forgave him he would spend the rest of his life making it up to me. Your advice was, "Forgive and forget. Trust him. He won't fail you." Well, I took your advice, and three months ago it happened again—this time in my own home with my dearest friend. I saw it coming but decided if he was one of those men who had to cheat I'd rather he cheat with someone I know and like. Here is the problem: My husband has been so ashamed since I caught them that he can't hold up his head in this woman's presence. He doesn't want her in our house ever again. Frankly, I like this woman very much. She is wonderful company and I hate to give up her friendship.—*M.I. Wrong*

Dear M.I.: The situation reminds me of that old joke: "My husband ran off with my best friend. What shall I do? I miss her." If you must continue the friendship, do so in the afternoon—at her house.

Dear Ann Landers: Emil and I have been married forty-five years. He is seventy-two and I am sixty-five. Emil has a lot of pep for a man his age, and everyone remarks on it. He is a good dancer and keeps up with all the latest steps. At parties he is a regular cutup, plays the harmonica, and does the soft-shoe. He likes to love me up in front of company, which everyone thinks is very sweet. But Emil doesn't stop there. When we are alone he still acts like a young colt, even though I've told him such foolishness is not proper for people our age. We have fourteen grandchildren, Ann. Don't you think it's time Grampa stopped acting like a movie Romeo? When I told him I wanted to write for your ideas, he said, "Go ahead and write. Ann Landers may give you the surprise of your life." I think he is wrong and that you will side with me. How about it? —Mrs. D

Dear Mrs. D: It is neither improper nor foolish. Why put a time limit on anything so precious as love and affection? If Emil is still making passes after forty-five years you should be bragging—not complaining.

Dear Ann Landers: I want to comment on the letter from the woman who was crushed by her husband's cheating. Your reply was right. You said the husband is "inadequate." What I want to know is this: Is there a husband left who plays it straight?

I was married many years to a man who cheated periodically. After each episode he would tell me he was sorry and vowed I was the only woman in the world who mattered. After a dozen indiscretions I lost all respect for him and finally we were divorced.

I then married a man who swore he was through running around and wanted one woman. Me. The first few years were heaven, but apparently life at home was too tame, and he began to seek outside excitement. I've given everything to this marriage and now there is nothing more to give.

I don't want to sound bitter, but I'm beginning to

believe that today *all* husbands are cheaters. When I recall the devotion and love between my father and mother, I wonder if love like theirs belonged to another generation.—*Disenchanted.*

Dear Disenchanted: Every generation has every kind of love.

There are fewer faithful husbands and wives today than there were fifty years ago simply because it is so much easier to cheat. Some of the reasons:

1. An unprecedented number of women are now working outside the home, and the temptations are multiplied.
2. Shorter working hours for everyone, more money, more leisure. This combination lends itself to mischief.
3. The world is shrinking, more men are traveling for business reasons. The husband who behaves in Boise may be unable to resist the temptation to slip his collar when he goes to Los Angeles.
4. Affairs have been glamourized by movies, novels, and TV. Divorce no longer carries the social stigma it once did. (Today 50 percent of the students enrolled at a California university come from broken homes.)

The cheating husband is insecure and needs to keep proving himself. The wise wife understands this. She doesn't rush to the divorce court, although she may well have more than adequate legal grounds.

Dear Ann Landers: I was amazed and disappointed with your advice to Sandy of Canada, the woman whose husband became amorous on the beach after their midnight swims. She said she had trouble getting him to the cottage and it was a real problem. Her question was, "Am I being prudish or is he getting nutty as he nears the foolish fifties?"

You told the woman that since you did not know how much privacy they had around their cottage, she'd better get him into the house "where he belongs."

As a fourth-generation Canadian I tell you that shuttered windows and tightly closed doors are a hangover from the mid-Victorian days when sex was considered evil. The reason so many husbands stray is because their brand of married love is routine, matter-of-fact, and downright boring.

A moonlit beach, a grassy slope, the sound of the wind whistling in the trees or the music of the surf beating on the shore, will add new excitement and a dimension of glamour to any marriage.

Please, Ann, don't be so conservative. Encourage married people to add some spice to their lovemaking. It could cut the divorce rate considerably.—*Your Neighbor To The North*

I thanked Neighbor To The North for her letter, but I scolded her for accusing me of being conservative. Through the years I have encouraged married couples who ask, to try everything in the book—and a few things that aren't.

Dear Ann Landers: I don't need advice. I need to unload. And maybe in the process I can wise up a few million women. Do you have a "best friend"? Forgive me if I plant a seed of suspicion, but the chances are good that your "best friend" is having an affair with your husband—or your wife. Couples are thrown together at parties and meetings. A spark is ignited. The woman with the roving eye develops a fondness for the man's wife. Soon the two couples are going everywhere together, even on trips, and a good time is had by all

—especially by two of them. This has happened to me three times, and I am now suffering through a fourth affair. My husband is a wonderful father and I think he loves me. The word "divorce" has never crossed his lips. Of course I'm crushed but I've resigned myself to waiting until he settles down or wears out, whichever happens first.—*Silent But Certain*

Dear Ann Landers: I received in the morning mail three copies of your column about the woman whose husband was having an affair with her best friend. The afternoon mail will be here at 3 P.M. There will probably be others. Why must people be so cruel? If I wish to pretend not to see my husband's faithlessness, whose business is it? I have four young children who need a father and I need a husband. I'm no good alone. For the past six years my husband has been having an affair with my best friend, an attractive widow. I'm sorrier for her than I am for myself. She's throwing herself away on a man who will never marry her. So, let this letter serve as an open reply to my "friends" who mailed me your column.—*Blind By Choice*

Dear Ann Landers: You and your big mouth. I telephoned my best friend this morning to ask if she had read your column. She replied, "Yes, and I think Ann Landers is crazy. I wouldn't have your husband if there was an atomic war and he was the only man left." This was a rotten insult and I really let her have it. Maybe you do a lot of good, but today you broke up a twelve-year friendship.—*Maxine*

Dear Maxine: Sorry about that.

Three

WHO'S IN CHARGE HERE ANYWAY?

If your children are beautifully adjusted, totally reliable, consistently obedient, cooperative, respectful, and have never caused you a moment's trouble, skip this chapter.

If, on the other hand, there are times when your children annoy you, exhaust you, worry you, and cause you to wonder what in heaven's name you're doing wrong, you may find in these pages a measure of solace and a few practical suggestions.

The embarrassing truth is that we live in a child-dominated society. The kids call the signals. They are in control.

When you see a family run by children, you will also see a set of embattled parents who are trying to buy love. What a sorry sight! And some of us need go no further than the mirror.

When we attempt to buy love the price goes up, as with other commodities. The child who senses that his parents feel guilty about leaving him with a sitter and a TV dinner will not hesitate to raise the price for "forgiveness." After he has collected his ransom, he will think of something else to be angry about so he can collect again. Emotional blackmail can be a profitable business, and there is no age limit. This game can be played from cradle to grave with considerable success.

My mail reflects the depressing spectacle of millions

of frightened and groveling parents, haunted by the ghosts of Adler and Freud, knocking themselves out to be "nice" to their offspring, trying to relate to them in Meaningful Ways, competing for approval, and making incredible financial sacrifices so their children will have every possible advantage—some never before heard of —outside the United States.

What the vast majority of American children needs is to stop being pampered, stop being indulged, stop being chauffeured, stop being catered to. In the final analysis it is not what you do for your children but what you have taught them to do for themselves that will make them successful human beings.

The following letters illustrate the point:

Dear Ann Landers: What can we do about a seventeen-year-old girl who stands in the center of the living room with a letter from Sarah Lawrence College in her hand and shrieks, "Sarah Lawrence doesn't want me! If I don't get into Stanford I'm going to marry Fatso!" All Patty's friends have the idea that if they aren't accepted by a "prestige" school, they'd rather not go anywhere. Some of Patty's friends have already blackmailed their parents into sending them to Europe for a year. Please don't say it's our fault, Ann. We've never given our daughter the impression that we prefer one school to another. In fact, there's a fine school 150 miles from here which would be much less costly than one of the Eastern schools. When we suggested it to Patty she screamed, "I'd rather die than go to that nothing college!" Your comments are invited.—*B. Wildered Parents*

Dear Parents: There are dozens of excellent small

schools, but they have no snob appeal, so unfortunately they go begging for students. High-school advisers can be enormously helpful in guiding students to select schools which are best suited to their emotional needs as well as well as their intellectual talents. Many a bright student accepted by an Ivy school is unable to cope with the competition. Such a student would be infinitely happier as the big fish in the small pond.

Dear Ann Landers: We have four normal children who are driving us abnormally crazy. The boys are stubborn and ornery. The girls are forever fighting and tormenting the neighbors. I say it's my wife's fault. Her idea of raising happy kids is to cater to them. She drives forty-five miles a day chauffeuring them to school and back, to dancing lessons, music lessons, and scout meetings. The neighbors complain because our children have ruined their flower beds, teased their dog, turned on their water faucets and flooded their lawn. I've told my wife she must stop pampering the kids. She says if children are allowed to get the deviltry out of their systems when they are young, they will grow up to be well-adjusted adults. How about this?
—*Pa*

Dear Pa: The kids will be lucky if the neighbors *let* them grow up. Where are you when all this nonsense goes on? These are your children, too, aren't they? Insist on some counseling. The school principal will direct you. Anyone who believes that undisciplined children are happy is mistaken. They are the saddest kids of all.

Dear Ann Landers: Our twenty-two-year-old daughter is engaged to a young man we know only slightly. This girl has finished college and has always shown good judgment—except in the selection of her fiancé.

The young man has an apartment in a bad section of town. He frequently phones our daughter and asks her to come to his place. She dashes out the door whenever he calls and never returns before midnight—always alone. My husband and I believe the young man should not ask her to come across town at night into a bad neighborhood and then allow her to go home alone. Are we old-fashioned? Should we speak up or remain silent?—*B. Cal.*

Dear B.: You aren't old-fashioned, you're just too late. Your daughter didn't get this way overnight. It's obvious she is so hungry for male attention that she will do anything to get it. As parents you have an obligation to speak up. Having spoken up, say no more. A girl twenty-two must (and probably will) make her own decision about when and where she will see her fiancé. A young man cannot respect a girl who has no *self*-respect. He demeans her by asking her to come to his place. And she degrades herself by going.

Dear Ann Landers: What's with parents, anyway? Don't they remember when they were kids? Why do they want to spare their children every hardship? We all have to face life sometime, so why don't they let us find out for ourselves? Teen-agers want to learn from experience and not be protected against everything. I am sixteen and my folks treat me like an infant. If I get into a jam or louse myself up it should be *my* problem. I'm only going to live once and I want to look back at all the fun I had and not remember my youth as a time when I couldn't do anything. Is it wrong to go where the other kids my age go, and do what they do?—*U. H. S. Student*

Dear Student: Where do the other kids go? And what do they do? If they go to dives where they can get liquor with faked ID cards you should *not* go there.

If they are sniffing glue or smoking marihuana or using goofballs or getting drunk, you should *not* be doing what they are doing. Certain things are best learned first-hand, but only a fool would jump off a cliff because he wanted to learn what's at the bottom. You say if you get loused up that's *your* problem. I have news for you. It's your parents' problem, too, because they are responsible for you.

Dear Ann Landers: Our son is sixteen years old, a fine student, and an obedient, respectful boy. After dinner his young friend Doug came over so they could study together. It was obvious that Doug was not speaking in a normal manner. He was talking louder than usual, slurring his words, and he also had the hiccups. I came right out and asked Doug if he had had a drink. He replied, "Yes, my father always offers me a highball when he has one. Tonight I had several." Then he added, "On the way over here I almost fell off my bicycle." My husband believes we should order our son to break off his friendship with Doug before he picks up some bad habits. Yes or no?—*Maple Leaf Mother*

Dear Mother: No. He may feel compelled to defend his buddy and stick with him. Keep expressing your faith in his integrity and his good judgment. Let him know you are confident that he will never disappoint you. Teen-agers have a truly magnificent way of living up to their parents' high opinion of them.

Dear Ann Landers: Do you want to be a national heroine? Please say something about mothers who bring small children to the beauty salon. I hire a sitter when I go to the beauty salon so that I can enjoy a few hours of quiet relaxation away from my own children. This represents quite an outlay of money for me, but I do it because I feel every woman should have some pet luxury.

It burns me up when other mothers spoil my afternoon because they are too cheap to hire a sitter. Operators hate it when kids fall over their feet, knock into manicuring tables, and mess up the rollers and hair clips. Of course they can't say anything. Will you please say it for them? Every shopowner and hairdresser in the world will love you.—*Hair Ye*

Dear Hair: Here's the letter and I hope it gets posted on a few thousand shampoo boards. Your sentiments are mine.

Dear Ann Landers: Here is an open letter to grandparents: Why, oh, why don't you treat your grandchildren the way you treated your own children when they were growing up? Did you stuff your own kids with ice cream, candy, and popcorn? Did you let them stay up beyond the normal bedtime just to have a little extra fun? Did you let your own kids talk back to you? Did you laugh at their bad manners and call it cute? Why then do this to your grandchildren?

We, the parents, have to undo all your spoiling when we take our children home from your place or after you leave our place. Please give your grandchildren a break. Stick to the rules their parents have set up for them. And please don't take your grandchild's side against his mom and dad. We have enough trouble raising kids today.

Thank you very much.—*Battle Weary Pensioneer*

Dear Pen: Some grandparents rationalize their permissiveness by saying, "We don't want to train our grandchildren, we want to enjoy them." This is extremely poor reasoning.

Grandparents undermine their children's hard work when they allow their grandchildren to get away with murder. And please don't say, "Wait until you have grandchildren of your own." I *have* grandchildren of my own, and I'm a pretty tough old cookie.

Dear Ann Landers: Our Barbara is almost two years old. She is very stubborn, and when she makes her mind up that's all there is to it. Barby used to refuse to eat vegetables or meat. The child was living on mashed potatoes, cake, candy, and cookies. She refused to drink milk unless I put chocolate syrup in it. I tried all sorts of tricks, like sprinkling sugar on the carrots, but it didn't work. She threw everything on the floor. Two weeks ago I was beside myself. I called our pediatrician. He said, "When you find out who is boss in your house call me back." And then he hung up. I was furious, then hurt. Later I began to think seriously about what he had said. I decided to *be* boss, and I set out that very day to serve Barby the food she should have. When she refused to eat it, I took it away. Later when she said she was hungry, I told her dinnertime was over. The next day it was the same story. By the third day Barby was so hungry she ate everything on her plate. The battle is over.—*The Winner*

Dear Winner: Hooray for you. But the best part of your story is that your child is the real winner. Kids who learn that they can tyrannize Mamma by refusing to eat often carry this mechanism into their adult lives, and they are a pain in the neck when they marry.

Dear Ann Landers: We are having the same family fight for the third summer in a row. Our son is now eleven and since he was nine, I (his father) have felt that Delbert should go to camp. He doesn't want to go, and his mother says there is no reason we should insist. I wouldn't mind if the boy did something constructive during the summer, but he stays up half the night watching TV and sleeps till noon. Then he nags his mother to take him swimming or to a movie. My wife says the child should not be forced to go to camp because he might feel rejected and this could damage his psyche for life. Your advice is wanted.—*The Singleton*

Dear Singleton: Your wife is raising a vegetable instead of a son, and you must share in the responsibility for whatever happens to him if you permit her to get away with it.

I received a speedy reply from the mother:

Dear Ann Landers: How dare you call my child a vegetable just because he refuses to go to camp? Did it ever occur to you that some children love their home and hate to leave it? And what's wrong with keeping kids home as long as possible? They grow up and leave too soon as it is. Delbert is a bright, sensitive boy. We sent him to camp two years ago when he was nine. After two days he telephoned and asked us to come get him. Delbert never was one to follow orders like sheep. I can tell by your writing, Ann Landers, that you have the mentality of a WAC sergeant. You like to boss people and impose your will on everybody. I'm raising my Delbert to be an independent thinker and a free soul in a free society. So phooey on you and your military approach to child rearing. This letter will never appear in print because you don't have a good answer.—*Proud Mum*

Dear Mum: Well, what d'ya know, here's your letter. But you are right, I have no answer, good or otherwise, for a reader who says phooey on me. Why try to reason with someone who won't listen? When Delbert runs into real trouble, don't hesitate to write, Mum. I'll try to help.

Dear Ann Landers: I am a mother whose heart is breaking. I raised eight children. My seventh child—a girl eighteen—just ran off and married a bum. We thought she would get tired of him or see for herself that he was no good, so we let them spend as much time together as they wanted. We even let her sleep weekends at his home, which we see now was a mistake. My husband and I think she is pregnant, and we blame the boy's parents. They should have kept an eye on them. I told off the boy's mother last week, and she ordered me out of her house. Our daughter heard about the incident, and now she won't speak to us. What can we do?—*Made Fools Of*

Dear Fools: Take turns kicking yourselves for letting your daughter run wild, and attempt to do a better job with your other children. It was *your* responsibility to guide the girl and to instill in her a sense of personal worth. Parents who allow a teen-age daughter to spend weekends at her boyfriend's home and then blame *his* parents because they didn't keep an eye on them are looking for a scapegoat.

Dear Ann Landers: When you finish reading this letter you'll probably say, "What a kook," and you are probably right. Maybe the menopause has something to do with it. My two sons are fifteen and eighteen. I love them very much—perhaps *too* much. It's the older boy I'm worried about. He always made excellent grades and was accepted by the college of his choice. He is thoughtful and kind and seems to be extremely attractive to girls. I know you'll say, "So what are you worrying about?" It's true, I don't have anything to worry about but I worry anyway. Particularly do I worry that he might take up drinking and be loose with girls. Most of his friends drink, and it scares me to death. I guess what I'm asking is how can I be relaxed about this boy and give him the freedom he deserves?—*Anxious Parent*

Dear Anxious: You've asked the $64,000 question: How does a mother cut her children loose—particularly a son? Your boy is eighteen. The job of molding his character, teaching him values, and instilling in him a sense of responsibility is done or it isn't done. If it isn't done, chances are that it never will be and worrying now won't help. The Bible said it best, "Train up a child in the way he should go: and when he is old he will not depart from it." That advice is as good today as it was two thousand years ago.

Dear Ann Landers: I am incensed by the advice you gave the young widow with the nine-year-old son. She said the boy was full of conversation at the dinner table and her father-in-law made the boy be quiet because he didn't approve of talking at the table. You said kids *should* talk at the table and suggested that the mother and son eat first and let the old man eat by himself if he wants silence. The trouble with kids today is they are all mouth. They run everything and everybody. They tell adults where to head in. They hit teachers and have no respect for authority. If a grandfather wants to discipline a boy by saying, "Shut up and eat—that's what you're at the table for," he should do it.—*Old-Fashioned Father*

Dear Old-Fashioned: Sorry, Dad, but I don't call "Shut up and eat" discipline. It's more like a dictatorship. Dinnertime should be family time. And family time means conversation involving all members of the family—small fry included.

Dear Ann Landers: I suppose you will say we got ourselves into this, and you are right, but we need help and we are counting on you to give it to us. Our sixteen-year-old daughter is an attractive, peppy, popular girl. In fact, she's *too* popular. She discovered the telephone at age fourteen. After that it became virtually impossible for anyone to get our line. Out of frustration we gave her a telephone of her own for Christmas. Almost immediately her grades began to slide. Her last report card was the worst. She almost flunked two subjects. Every night this week she has been on the phone till midnight. The telephone has become such an important part of her life, we are afraid to take it away from her. You once wrote, "A telephone is more than communication, it is an emotional outlet." Please tell us how to handle this.—*Frantic Parents*

Dear Frantic: Your daughter is obviously trying for permanent possession of the Bell Trophy. You'd better set up some controls at once. No teen-ager should be permitted to yak endlessly even if the phone *is* her own. Tell her the limit is one hour on school nights and two hours on weekends. She can spend all her time with one party, or she can talk to twelve different people. Let her know that if she breaks the rules you'll yank the phone.

Dear Ann Landers: I am twenty years old (boy) and have a driver's license but nothing to drive. For three years I have been asking my folks for a car. They say, "Go out and earn it." It is hard to get a job when you don't have a car. I've had six jobs since I dropped out of high school. None of them lasted very long. One of the problems is I can't get to work on time. If I had a car the problem would be solved. When I am working I give my folks fifteen dollars a week room and board. Now they don't get anything.

So you can see it would be better for them if they bought me a car, too. It isn't as if they can't afford it. Both my parents are working and together they make $12,000 a year. I am not asking for a Rolls-Royce. Any make will do. Please give me a hand.—*Need Wheels*

Dear Wheels: A kid who can't get to work on time on public transportation is not likely to do better if he has his own car. He'd probably do worse. My advice: Forget about a car and concentrate on a high-school diploma. Either go back to school or take night courses. Dropouts are a problem to society, to their families, and to themselves. Right now you need education—not wheels.

Dear Ann Landers: Our children are seven and nine years of age. They love to watch TV. My wife thinks this is great because it keeps them out of her hair. After dinner the children sit in front of the set until they can't see straight. When I tell my wife to put the kids to bed she says, "They will go when they get tired." They end up falling asleep on the floor. I have to undress them and carry them upstairs. This goes on night after night. My wife sees nothing wrong with it. What do you say?—*One Against Three*

Another reader suggested a solution:

Dear Ann: This is how we solved the TV problem in our family: We sat down with our kids and admitted we had left too much decision-making up to them. We announced there would be new rules and regulations and they would have to stick to them. We set up a bedtime schedule. Sample: The seven-year-old should be in bed at 8:00 P.M. and the nine-year-old at 8:30. And don't take any lip. The next step is a tough one because it requires some giving on Mother's part. Keep the TV off for several days, even if it means missing some of your favorite programs—or Dad's. (You'll need his help with this.) Then sit down and read with your children. Play chess, put on some good records. Help them discover the world beyond the idiot-box. Allow them to resume their TV viewing with a fresh outlook—schoolwork and chores completed— and *you* decide what's worth watching. Don't expect success without plenty of sweating, Mother. And don't try it at all unless you have the guts.—*Judy W.*

Dear Ann Landers: I am twelve years old, and although I am not smart I have learned a few things that some parents have not learned yet. When I was younger and my mom or dad said to me, "You can't have that," I would get mad and say to myself, "Boy, they are mean! When I have children of my own I'm going to buy them everything they want so they will be happy." Two weeks ago my sister Barbara came to visit and brought her children. Barbara's husband is rich, and the kids are spoiled and don't appreciate anything. They break their toys as fast as they get them, and then they start on the furniture. They are big complainers and cry a lot. They don't mind worth a hoot. My sister Libby's kids are exactly the opposite. They don't get many toys, but they are tickled to death with whatever they get. They take good care of their belongings and never seem to break anything. Libby's kids hardly ever cry and seem happy all the time. They mind their parents and are respectful to other people. Also, they are good to each other, and Barbara's kids are like killing each other ten times a day. Now I know why kids get spoiled, and I am going to raise my children to be like Libby's.—*Miss Watcher*

Dear Miss: You are smarter at twelve than most

mothers are at thirty-five. When the time comes, I hope you will practice what you are preaching today.

Dear Ann Landers: We have five children who are normal, healthy, and well-behaved, thanks to the firm handling of my husband and my own belief that parents need not take any sass or nonsense. Sunday we were visiting in the home of my husband's brother and his wife. They have three boys who do as they please. There isn't one piece of furniture in their home that isn't broken. The floors are scratched because the kids slide in their golf shoes. Holes have been punched in the wall by the boys on their tricycles. The seven-year-old asked my husband if he could take his shoes off and walk in them. My husband said, "No." The boy asked, "Why not?" My husband replied, "Because my shoes are not toys." The youngster said, "If you don't let me I'll sock you." My husband said, "You'd better not." The boy struck my husband in the back with his fist and ran to his father. My husband got up and gave the child a hard swat on the rear. The boy's father was furious. He shouted, "You have no right to strike my son. If you want to beat your own kids that's *your* business, but our children are not accustomed to violence." An argument followed and we left on strained terms. May I have your opinion? Frankly, I have mixed emotions. Please direct your remarks to my husband. Thank you.—*Q.T.*

Dear Q.T.: I have only two words for your husband: Heartiest congratulations.

Four

IS THERE A DOCTOR IN THE HOUSE?

Leading authorities in the field of mental health tell us that at least 60 percent of the patients in hospital beds today are there because of an illness which was triggered by an emotional problem. Add to that figure the patients who jam waiting rooms of physicians' offices, hoping the doctor can give them "something" to "make them feel better."

Include, please, the insomniacs, the accident prone, and the nervous wrecks who have made the tranquilizer industry a fifty million dollar a year business.

Don't stop here. The picture is incomplete without the ulcer patients, the migraine sufferers, and those who are plagued with chronic skin problems caused by "nerves."

For centuries man has known it is impossible to separate the body from the mind. What transpires in the head is bound to produce a physical reaction. The simple act of blushing is a dramatic example. Fainting at the sight of blood is another.

People who write to me about emotional problems frequently describe physical aches and pains without realizing there might be a connection. For example: "My husband's drinking is doing terrible things to our marriage. I walk the floor at night wondering if he is in a ditch somewhere. In addition to worrying about my husband I've been bothered lately with blistering head-aches."

And this from a teen-ager: "My boyfriend and I started to go steady last January. One thing led to another and this summer we went all the way. What we are doing is against my religion. I know I am sinning but just can't control myself. After we say good night I get terrible stomachaches—probably from eating junk after supper."

Thirty-five years ago we used to lock mentally ill relatives in the attic. We've come a long way, but we have miles to go. Too many people still believe mental illness is a sign of weakness or inadequacy or failure —something to be ashamed of. Nothing could be further from the truth.

Statistics indicate that the percentage of breakdowns is greater among the better educated, and the achievers. The experts tell us, too, that we inherit our nervous systems. So it stands to reason that one who comes from a family of Nervous Nancys might have a more difficult time coping with life's problems.

No one feels ashamed or defensive about a ruptured disc or kidney stones, but if a doctor tells a patient his skin ailment is caused by an emotional problem and suggests psychiatric help, the patient might shop around for a doctor who will tell him he has an allergy, since this is easier to explain to friends and relatives.

In my column I have tried to help readers recognize the link between their emotional problems and their physical ailments. This is not to suggest that every ache and pain is caused by anger, fear, frustration, or worry, but there is sufficient evidence to support the statement that at least half of them are.

In the past thirteen years I have urged thousands of people to get counseling or psychiatric help. I know of course that in some cases this advice is useless. Therapy will not produce results for everyone. Some individuals are too rigid, their problems are too deeply imbedded, they are incapable of surrendering their neurotic dependencies. And sometimes the failure lies with the therapist. If a writer tells me he is making no progress, that he does not get on well with his therapist and sees no point in continuing, I urge him to try another therapist. A competent doctor will be happy to assist in the change.

I have been accused of copping out because I frequently advise my readers to "get professional help." While this may appear to be buck-passing it is excellent advice. I cannot in a single paragraph unsnarl a life that has been messed up for thirty years. A great many people need counseling on a continuing basis— someone who will listen to their agonies and hostilities and resentments. Many clergymen are splendid counselors and some physicians will take the time to listen, but the demands of their daily responsibilities often make it impossible to give a single individual the time he needs to discuss, on a continuing basis, the things that are bothering him.

The most rewarding letters I receive are from those to whom I have suggested psychiatric help. Here is an excerpt: "Two years ago when I first wrote to you I was considering suicide. My marriage was a shambles, my children were out of control, and my mother was driving me crazy. I wanted to go to sleep and never wake up. I wrote to you one night because I had come to the end of my rope.

"Your answer changed my life. You told me I had responsibilities to live up to—to stop feeling sorry for myself and to shape up. You said, 'If you can't do it yourself, see a psychiatrist.' I took your advice and today I am a new woman—a better woman than I ever dreamed I could be. It was as if someone raised the shades and let the light into my life. I now know where I have been—and where I am going."

Dear Ann Landers: My steady boyfriend just gave me my engagement ring. This means I must go to a doctor for a premarital physical examination. I don't mind going to a doctor to have my throat painted or to get a flu shot, but the thought of a physical examination by a man makes me sick to my stomach. Please, Ann, don't tell me I'm afraid of men and to get over my prudishness before I marry or I will be in trouble. The truth is, my boyfriend and I have already done things you don't approve of—so it isn't that. And don't suggest a woman doctor. There isn't one in this town. I want to overcome this terrible feeling, because I'll be faced with it again when I have children. Can you help me?—*The Shakes*

Dear Shakes: I don't know what you think you have that is so different, but don't feel hurt if the doctor doesn't notice. A nurse will probably be present during the examination and you will be draped in sheets and it won't be half as bad as you imagine. Get going.

Dear Ann Landers: Your statement to the young girl who dreaded being examined by a doctor was absurd. The notion that physicians are immune to the charms of attractive female patients is extremely naïve. As an attorney who has listened to countless complaints about physicians who have behaved in a questionable manner during physicial examinations, I hope you will read up a little before you make any more such stupid statements. A great deal of hanky-panky goes on in the examining rooms of physicians, both during and after office hours. Anyone who thinks otherwise is just not tuned in to the times.—*Mr. 720*

Dear Mr.: Since there are approximately 250,000 physicians in the country, one must expect a few dingbats. I doubt that the percentage of swingers is higher among medics than any other group, however. The following letter should be of interest to you.

Dear Ann Landers: My husband is a physician, fifty-two years of age, pleasant-looking but far from handsome. He is a gentle person and I can understand why patients confide in him. What astonishes me, however, is the number of women patients who have come right out and asked him to have sexual relations. In the last six months there were three. One was a beautiful young widow who felt the doctor should provide her with sex as a form of therapy. She said she would not consider it anything "personal" but rather a treatment for her nerves. She would, of course, expect to be billed. Another was a married woman whose husband was impotent. She said the doctor would be performing a humanitarian service by preventing her from becoming promiscuous. The third was a high-school girl (age sixteen) who felt her first sex experience should be with an older man who "knew what he was doing." I have talked to wives of other physicians and they get the same offers. Occasionally you publish a letter from a woman who complains about a doctor making indecent proposals in the office. I thought you might like to get an accurate picture from one who knows.—*M.D.'s Wife*

Dear Ann Landers: My brother wrote me a nasty letter two years ago and said I was responsible for his wife's nervous breakdown. I admit I never cared for Emma and I did needle her a little, but I refuse to accept responsibility for her nervous breakdown. This morning I received a phone call from my brother. He said, "I just wanted you to know that Emma is going to be operated on for varicose veins tomorrow and it's your fault." I asked him how he figured I was to blame for Emma's varicose veins, and he replied, "The doctor said depression affects the capillaries, and there is no doubt that the unhappiness you have caused Emma has brought on this varicose condition." Emma has had five children in six years, and I think *this* is what caused her varicose veins. Check with your medical authorities and let me know if I am right.—*Not Guilty*

Dear Not: A woman who has five children in six years is a fairly good prospect for varicose veins even if she has a sister-in-law who is crazy about her. Ignore your brother's accusation and send Emma a nice bouquet of flowers. This type of surgery is no fun.

Dear Ann Landers: Last evening in the presence of guests Mother began to relate the details of her recent operation. When she reached into her handbag and took out a jar which contained her gallstones, I couldn't believe it. My husband was horrified. The guests were courteous, but I could see stricken looks as they handed the bottle of gallstones from one to the other. After the guests left I suggested to Mother that she'd better not pass around the exhibit again because some folks might consider it offensive. Mother said, "You are wrong. It is educational. Most folks live a lifetime and never get to see a gallstone."—*Mary*

Dear Mary: Come to think of it I've never seen a gallstone, and if I *never* see one it will be just fine. Few topics are more tiresome than the details of someone else's operation. The "exhibit" is OK for pre-med students, but it has no place in the living room.

Dear Ann Landers: Several days ago I awakened at about 2 A.M. with a headache. I went to the bathroom to get an aspirin and fell. I was sure I had broken my shoulder. My husband telephoned his young cousin who has just started to practice medicine. He came right over and said he didn't think it was a fracture but advised me to get X rays the next morning. He gave me a sleeping pill. I had the X rays taken and there was no fracture. This morning I received a bill for the X rays ($35) and a bill from my husband's cousin for $15. I don't mind paying for the X rays but that young whippersnapper had a nerve charging me $15 for a sleeping pill. Had we known he was going to send a bill, we would have called our regular family doctor. We just wanted to give the boy a break and help him get some practical experience. Were we wrong?—*Tennessee*

Dear Tenn: Just what kind of a break is it for a doctor (young or old) to make a house call at 2 A.M. for nix? Doctors get plenty of practical experience taking care of fathers, mothers, sisters, brothers, nieces, nephews, and grandparents for free—not to mention charity cases and clinic patients. Internship also offers a world of free experience, particularly the odd-hour variety. Pay the bill and do your cousin a favor by not giving him any more breaks in the middle of the night.

Dear Ann Landers: I am a sixteen-year-old girl. My best friend is sixteen also. Last night, Wendy was at my house and suddenly she said, "How can I get bronchial pneumonia?" I asked her why in the world she wanted to get bronchial pneumonia. She answered, "Oh, I don't want to die or anything. I'd just like to get sick enough to go to the hospital so people will send me cards and flowers and the fellows will visit me and see me in my nightgown with my hair loose." I was shocked at her idea of fun. Have you ever heard of anything so far out? Is Wendy crazy or what? Thanks for your help.—*Can't Dig It*

Dear Can't Dig: Anyone who has had bronchial

pneumonia will tell you it's no fun. But, of course, Wendy doesn't really want to be sick, she just wants the fringe benefits. Illness is a surefire attention-getter. Moreover, it provides a respectable excuse for not going to school or to work. You'd be surprised at the number of people who resort to this technique.

Dear Ann Landers: I announced my engagement to this man a year ago last December. We are not children, Ann; we are both in our late twenties. We've kept steady company for three years. The wedding date has been set four times. Each time it had to be postponed. Eight days before the wedding he broke his leg and we had to cancel everything. Two months later he developed a mysterious fever and was hospitalized; this was six days before the wedding. The following month the date was set for the 15th. On the 10th he suddenly lost his hearing and had to fly East to see a specialist. Last week we were all set when his mother broke out with giant hives. He now says we can't be married until his mother recovers. I'd like your ideas. —Wilted Bouquet

Dear Wilted: This man's subconscious (and his mother) are protecting him against a marriage he doesn't want. If you succeed in becoming his wife (during an attack of good health), you'll probably regret it.

Dear Ann: Is it thoughtlessness, stupidity, cruelty, ignorance, or just plain nosiness that makes people ask members of the family, "Was it cancer?" My father had surgery a few days ago. The surgeon gave us bad news. My mother is heartsick and so am I. We are trying to be brave—and silent—but people won't let us. They keep badgering us with questions. Yesterday I received six telephone calls, all from friends wanting to know details. I've been saying, "We are hoping for the best," because I don't want to discuss it. One caller said, "You might as well face facts. It will be easier later." Another caller said, "My mother died of cancer and I pity you. You'll go through hell these next few months." Why do people do this? What should I say? —*Near The Edge*

Dear Near: Real friends don't push the bounds of good taste by asking questions. Cassandra types and those who feed on the misery of others are not friends. They are clods.

Dear Ann Landers: Maybe I'm a nut but my blood pressure zooms about fifty points when I see my wife smoke a cigarette. I am not opposed to smoking on moral grounds, but some women look terrible when they smoke and my wife looks worse than most. The cigarette just dangles in the corner of her mouth like the house man in a 21 game. When the smoke curls up into her face, she squints her eyes and the mascara runs. Nora smokes filter tips. Sometimes she absent-mindedly lights up the wrong end of the cigarette, and the house smells like the wind is coming from the packing house in Omaha. I don't want to get into a thing with Nora about smoking, but I wish she'd quit. Do you think I have the right to ask her?—*Nora's Mate*

Dear Mate: Of course. And she has the right to do as she pleases. If a woman doesn't mind discoloring her teeth, fouling her breath, smelling up her hair, setting fire to a few hundred dollars every year, burning small holes in her clothes and the furniture, and finally, if she chooses to ignore the evidence that there is a link between lung cancer and cigarette smoking—well, that's her business.

Dear Ann Landers: Please tell me what to do about a woman twenty-seven years old who has a chronic respiratory ailment and is thirty-five pounds over-weight. She smokes like a chimney and eats everything in sight. She "forgets" to take her medicine even though her doctor has told her she is a very sick girl and it is essential that she follow his orders. I am especially concerned because I am the doctor and the young woman is my daughter. If this patient were a stranger to me, I would wipe my hands of the case, but how can I abandon my own child? Please give me some advice. I am alternately furious and depressed over this frustrating situation.—*St. Louis M.D.*

Dear Doctor: If you want your daughter to live, you'd better pretend she is someone else's daughter and wipe your hands of the case. Give her a list of three physicians and tell her to select one. This young woman is using her illness as a weapon. She is determined to ignore your orders, and do as she pleases if it kills her. And it might—if you continue as her physician.

Dear Ann Landers: My cousin is engaged to marry a chiropodist. She introduces him as Dr. Ingemar Strudelgrubber, which, of course, is not his real name. Her emphasis is on the word "doctor" to give the impression he is a brain surgeon or something. I think it would be more honest if she introduced him as Ingemar Strudelgrubber and added, "He is a chiropodist." What is your opinion?—*Just Asking*

Dear Asking: A chiropodist is a foot doctor who has earned the professional title. He doesn't need to be a brain surgeon to be called doctor. So your cousin can go right ahead and introduce her fiancé as Dr. Ingemar Strudelgrubber—and I'm happy it's not his real name, too.

Dear Ann Landers: What do you think of a husband who wakes his wife up at 2:00 A.M. to tell her to stop snoring? Clem started this a few months ago when he retired from his job. I am *not* retired, however. Clem can sleep late in the morning but I can't. Last night when Clem woke me up I got real mad. I asked him what in the world he thought he was accomplishing. He said, "Nothing is more annoying than to be kept awake by a snorer. The snorer should stay up and keep his victim company." Isn't this the meanest thing you ever heard of? I do not snore on purpose. If I could stop I would. What can I do?—*Pooped*

Dear Pooped: See a doctor and learn if he can do anything about your snoring. Sometimes minor surgery will eliminate the problem. If the doctor says it is more complicated in your case, buy a cot and sleep in another part of the house.

Dear Ann Landers: Please say a word to the smug, self-satisfied dames who think they deserve a medal because they gain so little weight during pregnancy that they don't even have to buy maternity clothes. How a woman carries the baby depends on the way she's built. A woman can't choose her bone structure any more than she can choose the color of her eyes. With my first baby I gained only eleven pounds, but I was so enormous that our friends were taking bets it would be twins for sure and maybe triplets. My sister-in-law gained twenty-seven pounds, and nobody knew she was pregnant until she was due to go to the hospital. So, please, Ann, tell that obnoxious dame not to be so proud of herself. It's all in the lap of the gods.— *Mother Hood*

Dear Mother: It's also in the lap of the ladies—and some ladies don't see their laps for six months because they use pregnancy as an excuse to eat everything in sight. The build is important, but the gal who eats sensibly and keeps her weight down will look better—and she'll feel better, too.

Dear Ann: I'm thirty-two, have been married for three years, and both my husband and I want a family awfully bad. The problem is that I am petrified of childbirth. Whenever a friend tells me she is pregnant, I become so envious I can hardly stand it. Then I get to thinking about the agony of labor pains, and I'm glad it's not me. The conflict is terrible, and I don't know what to do about it. I know I'm being unfair to my husband, and this has caused terrible guilt feelings. Is there any hope for me?—*Childless*

Dear Childless: There are over three billion people in the world and every single one of them got here the same way. Some women have prolonged and excruciating deliveries. Other women have had such speedy deliveries that their babies are born in taxis, in hospital corridors, and in elevators. Make an appointment with an obstetrician and discuss your anxieties. He will describe the various types of anesthesia which should give you reassurance. Look at it this way: If you had an attack of appendicitis, you'd have the bellyache and nothing to show for it.

Dear Ann Landers: The other evening my husband said to me, "Did you take your pill, dear?" I replied, "You mean *our* pill, don't you? After all, The Pill is a family affair." He looked at me as if I had taken leave of my senses.

My husband is typical of the newly liberated male. To my way of thinking the American husband never did accept his share of responsibility in regard to sex and pregnancy. Now that we have The Pill the husband just plain doesn't want to be bothered with anything. The only thing on his mind is did *she* remember to take *her* pill.

Several months ago I read about a birth control pill for men. So far as I know *that* pill has never been perfected. And you can be sure it won't be since most medical research is done by men and they will continue to shunt the responsibility off on the female.

We women are partly to blame because we have allowed the men to get away with it. I remember last year an unmarried career girl wrote and asked if her gentleman friend should share in the cost of The Pill. (She was reluctant to ask him because she "didn't know him well enough to talk about money.")

So please, Ann Landers, help liberate the long-suffering female by printing this letter.—*Frailty Thy Name*

Dear Frail: When a woman takes a pill it's *her* pill, whether it's an aspirin, a vitamin, or what have you—so stop trying to make it a family affair, lady.

Dear Ann Landers: I have been married three years, and my problem is getting worse instead of better. My husband and I get along fine when there are just the two of us, but when we are with family or friends, I get dizzy spells and my heart begins to pound like a trip hammer. Sometimes my stomach gets tied up in knots and I become nauseated and can't eat. When I am with these same people and my husband is not present, I enjoy myself and feel just fine. I should tell you that my husband was not born in this country and his ways are a little different. My parents were opposed to our marriage, but now they have accepted him. I've told myself that he is doing his best, and I am no longer ashamed of the way he speaks. I've gone to a heart specialist, and he says my heart is fine. What is the matter with me?—*Wee Sally*

Dear Wee: You are probably having anxiety symptoms because of your unconscious feelings about your husband. Some people go through life half-sick, dizzy, heart pounding, stomach in knots, without realizing that their physical discomfort comes from unrelieved tension. You need outside help. Go to your family doctor for a complete physical checkup and ask him to direct you.

Dear Ann Landers: I've been a widow for five years. When my husband died I never dreamed I could ever be interested in another man. But the wounds have healed. I am forty-eight years old and look every day of it. My figure is trim, and with the help of a beautician I've kept the gray out of my hair. But it's the small pouches under my eyes and my sagging jowls that give me away. If I had a little surgery, I would look ten years younger. When I see the attractive divorcees who have youth and beauty on their side, I realize the competition is razor sharp. The woman who looks thirty-eight is sure to get more chances than the woman who looks forty-eight. Be realistic, Ann, do I see the plastic surgeon or not?—*Mirrors Don't Lie*

Dear M.: The man who is interested in worthwhile human literature will read between the lines. Have the surgery if you think it will lift your spirits, but don't expect it to produce miracles. And P.S.: A man who would be attracted to a woman because she looks a few years younger is no red-hot bargain.

Dear Ann Landers: My husband is 6'3" and he says he weighs 265 pounds, but I don't believe it. He refuses to get on a scale in my presence. I had him on a special diet but gave up when I discovered the diet meal was just a snack, and he was eating everything in sight when my back was turned. The children hide their candy from him, but he finds it. When I bake for my club he sneaks into the freezer and eats the desserts. I think he has high blood pressure, but he won't go to a doctor. You told the other wife that some things are worth nagging about and a husband's health is one of them. Does this go for me, too?—*Open For Suggestions*

Dear Open: Yes, but change your tune. Tomorrow tell him you are making an appointment with a doctor. Ask which day and what time would be best. If he fails to cooperate, ask if his affairs are in order because he will probably not be around to see his children through college. And neither will the husbands of the women who wrote the next two letters.

Dear Ann Landers: Steve is a fifty-two-year-old, hardhitting, driven businessman. We have a lovely home and a fine family, but he is too busy to notice. When the stock market goes down a quarter of a point, he notices *that,* however. Three years ago Steve had a serious heart attack. His doctors told him he must lose forty pounds and quit smoking. He hasn't lost an ounce and he smokes more than ever. He has had diabetes for ten years and is all right when he remembers to take his medicine. When he doesn't remember he goes into shock. This has happened twice in the last six months. I've begged, pleaded, threatened, cried, but nothing fazes him. He still eats whatever he wants, smokes, drinks too much, and works fourteen hours a day. What can I do with a man like this?—*Nervous Wreck*

Dear Wreck: Nothing. But you can do something for yourself and your family. See that his insurance is in order, and check with his lawyer to make certain he has made a will.

Dear Ann Landers: My husband who is forty-one has had a serious liver problem for over seven years. This last year it has become much worse. The doctor told Jack in 1959 that he must give up alcohol if he wants to live. I have threatened to leave him, I've cried, and even gotten down on my knees and begged him to leave liquor alone, but I might as well talk to the lamppost. Two weeks ago, Jack had an acute attack and had to be rushed to the hospital. I thought surely it would kill him or cure him. Lord knows how he pulled through. Jack has been home from the hospital three days and is feeling much better. Tonight before supper he fixed himself a Martini. Now he's on his fourth and doesn't want to eat at all. Why would a man do this when his doctor has told him it adds up to suicide?—*Despondent Wife*

Dear Wife: Because he is an alcoholic. And alcoholics want to kill themselves, but they'd rather use a bottle than a gun.

Dear Ann: Without realizing it, you are educating a great many people—even those who insist at the top of their lungs that they are reading you for laughs. Will you please say a few words about menopause? I am forty-seven years old. (Everyone who writes to you says, "I look younger." Well, not me. *I* look older.) For the past two years, I've had hot flashes and sinking spells. During supper, I will say, "Joe, open the window. I'm burning up." Twenty minutes later, I'll say, "Joe, close the window. I'm freezing." He tells me I am imagining things and that I am off my rocker. Will you please print in your column that this is part of the menopause?—*28 Years Of Service*

Dear 28: Hot flashes are indeed a part of the menopause. An enlightened and sympathetic husband can do a great deal to help a woman over this difficult time of her life. A visit with a doctor can also help. Medication is now available so that women don't have to suffer as their mothers did thirty years ago.

I get a lot of letters like this one from another menopausal lady:

Dear Ann Landers: Please tell all men around fifty years of age that they could save themselves a lot of money on doctor bills if once in a while they would tell their wives they love them. Going through the change doesn't bother a woman much if she has a thoughtful, considerate husband. The change is a normal transition. Some of my friends have sailed through it beautifully. With me, it's another story. My husband is always telling me about this woman's shape and that one's sexy walk. Every time an attractive girl waits on us in a restaurant his eyes bug out of his head. I see a doctor every week for shots and pills. It's easier to blame the change than to admit I'm depressed because my husband makes me feel like an old bag. I'll bet thousands of other women are in this same lousy boat. —*Discarded*

Dear Discarded: The menopause is unquestionably harder on some women than others. It can also produce emotional changes—depression and suspicion. A thoughtful, considerate husband, however, can help. The wife who feels she's over the hill is bound to have a rougher time.

Dear Ann Landers: You said in a recent column an enlightened husband can be a great help to his wife during the menopause. Well, I'd like to add that an enlightened woman can also help herself—if she wants to. My wife's mother is a classic example of a woman who has used the menopause for all it's worth. She is sixty-eight and has kept her husband hovering over her with a fan in one hand and a sweater in the other for twenty years. Whenever she insults a friend (which is often) she says, "The change has made me awfully nervous." My own mother takes her pills quietly, goes to the doctor for shots, and you never hear a word out of her. My wife has already promised me that when this happens to her she is going to keep her mouth shut, and I am—*Grateful.*

Dear Grateful: A woman of sixty-eight who has been complaining about the menopause for twenty years is overdoing it. She should have rung down the final curtain on that performance long ago. It's always pathetic when people must use physical discomfort (real or imaginary) as an attention-getting device. This in itself is a sickness, so don't be too hard on the old girl.

Dear Ann Landers: I'm dictating this letter to the nurse because I'm not yet able to sit up and hold a pencil. Please print my letter for other executives who think they can't possibly spare the time to take a vacation. Suddenly I have plenty of time, but all I can do is lie flat on my back and look at the ceiling. The doctor won't even let me make a phone call. He says I'm lucky to be alive after that massive heart attack. I thought my company would collapse if I didn't get to the office every morning at 8 A.M. At night I always lugged work home. I never took time to have lunch with a friend. I used to grab a sandwich at my desk and dictate to my secretary between bites. I drove my associates crazy, telephoning them at crazy hours and on Sundays. I could never spare the time to see a movie or a play or just sit around with friends. I had too much to do. For the last five years, my wife has been begging me to go to a doctor and get a physical, but I couldn't spare the time. Now I discover the business is doing fine without me—in fact, the figures are up. If God gives me a few more years, I'll know how to use them. Strange that a man has to look death in the face before he learns how to live.—*Six-Figure Idiot*

Dear Ann Landers: A dear friend of mine has had a horrible experience. Emily (not her real name) noticed a lump in her breast. She went to a physician and was told to check into the hospital for surgery that evening. The operation was performed within forty-eight hours. When Emily awoke from the anesthetic she learned that her breast had been removed. She went into a deep depression (which I understand is not unusual), but she began to cheer up on the fourth day. On the fifth day, however, it leaked out that the biopsy report on the amputated breast was negative. This made the poor woman so furious that she just about tore the hospital apart. What can be done to prevent such catastrophes in the future? Don't suggest that Emily sue the doctor. Everyone knows the medical profession is such a tightly knit little group that it's ridiculous to try to fight them.—*California Yell For Help*

Dear California: Like most secondhand reports, your story contains serious flaws. No reputable physician removes a breast unless he first does a biopsy on the lump and finds a malignancy. This procedure is standard and virtually eliminates the possibility of removing a healthy breast. Furthermore, all certified hospitals are required by the American Hospital Association and the American College of Surgeons to maintain an examining body called a tissue committee. This committee reviews reports describing all organs which have been removed. Years ago a surgeon could remove just about anything and not have to answer to anyone. Today if a doctor chalked up an unseemly number of unnecessary operations, he would be dropped from the hospital staff.

Dear Ann Landers: I resent your sarcastic reply to California Yell For Help, the woman who lashed out at the surgeon who removed her friend's healthy breast. According to you, it simply could not have happened. You said all surgeons must do a biopsy first and that no reputable physician would perform such an operation unless the biopsy showed a malignancy.

You as much as called the woman a liar. May I direct your attention to the word "reputable." I would not argue the point that the majority of physicians are reasonably honest, some are highly principled, and a few are totally dedicated, but that still leaves a number of knife-hungry scroundrels, not to mention chronic alcoholics who bury their mistakes and no one is any the wiser. So please, Ann Landers, don't try to give the public the impression that every physician who hangs out a shingle is incapable of error. Tell it like it is.— *Calling Dr. Kildare*

Dear Calling: There are incompetents, phonies, and bad actors in every field, and the medical profession is no exception. Unfortunately when a physician is unscrupulous or botches a job, someone becomes severely ill or dies. I know of no profession, however, that does such a conscientious job of policing its own members. Peer approval among physicians is of utmost importance. Medical organizations, county, state, and national, are persistent and diligent in their fight against charlatans and quacks. Medical standards are constantly being elevated by medical audit committees in the nation's hospitals. Additional safeguards are provided by tightening the requirements for hospital certification involving total patient care. When one considers that before the Abraham Flexner Report in 1910, "doctors" in some states were permitted to practice medicine by virtue of a certificate purchased for as little as five dollars, I say the medical profession has made enormous strides. All professions should do as well.

Dear Ann Landers: I just finished the column in which you staunchly defend the medical profession. You very politely say that no human is infallible and that, unfortunately, when a physician makes a mistake somebody becomes severely ill or dies. This is advice?

I am enclosing in my letter to you a clipping from the London *Sunday Times*. It reports one of the most interesting errors of all time. A surgeon in Birmingham, England, amputated the wrong leg. I agree with you, Ann, that no human is infallible, and I can understand certain kinds of "mistakes," but *this* is ridiculous. Have you the courage and decency to print my letter?—*San Jose Reader*

Dear Jose: Thank you for your letter and for the clipping. Outrageous mistake? Unquestionably so. But the comments of the seventy-five-year-old widow who is now legless were far more deserving of notice than the doctor's mistake. She said, "Whoever it was who made the operating error probably saved hundreds of lives before he got to me. I happened to be the unlucky one. But as I told them at the time, we all make mistakes, and I am not going to have one word said against him." What a sterling example of charity! That this woman was able not only to forgive but to defend the man, is mercy in its best sense. Thank you for sending me the clipping. It contained something of value for all of us.

Dear Ann Landers: After I spent several hundred dollars to come to this world-famous medical center in Minnesota, the doctors had the nerve to tell me I am not sick. The final consultation took one hour. My X rays and previous history going back ten years were hauled out. The doctor ended the consultation by saying, "You are in good physical condition for a woman your age. Go home and find something to keep yourself busy." What he meant was, "You are healthy as a horse but you are nuts." When doctors can't get to the root of the trouble, why do they tell the patient his troubles are imaginary?—*Ill But Undiagnosed*

Dear Ill: Lady, I feel sorry for you. You will now go from doctor to doctor, shopping around until somebody sells you an operation. But that won't be the end of it. You will then complain about your adhesions. Your pain is not imaginary. It is real but it is probably caused by anxiety, tension, and unresolved problems. This is what your doctor tried to tell you. Only if you get your emotional machinery in good running condition will you feel better.

Dear Ann Landers: I am a boy, sixteen, who thinks you are the grooviest. I need your help, and I hope you'll come through. At first it was just a few pimples, but now my face and neck are covered. My mother says it is part of growing up and I shouldn't let it bother me. She keeps telling me time will take care of it. For over a year, I have been self-conscious and miserable. How much longer should it take? I have tried laying off certain foods, but it hasn't helped. I bought medicines I saw advertised, and they haven't done me any good. We don't have a lot of money for doctors, so please don't suggest treatments. Should I keep trying the medicines in hopes something will help, or should I be patient and hope time will take care of it? Do you know of any cure?—*The New Orleans Mess*

Dear New Orleans: There is no sure cure for acne. A treatment that works wonders for one person might prove totally worthless for another. Go to a doctor. You don't need "a lot of money." You will spend less with a good doctor than if you continue to buy worthless concoctions and treat yourself. Special lamp treatments (in the physician's office, of course) have helped thousands of kids just like you. Please make an appointment today.

Dear Ann Landers: At what age should a daughter be allowed to go into a doctor's examining room without her mother? I am fourteen years old and mature for my age. My mother has always been too protective and domineering. We had a great big argument over this, and she made me feel like a fool. The doctor told my mother (in my presence) that it was not necessary for her to stay with me during the examination, but she raised such a fuss he finally let her have her way. Please reply in the paper for the benefit of other girls who may have this problem.—*Overruled Daughter*

Dear Daughter: Any child who is old enough to walk is old enough to go into a physician's examining room without Mother. Most doctors have a nurse to assist them, so you would in all probability not have been alone. It's unfortunate that the doctor did not overrule your mother instead of allowing her to overrule him.

Dear Ann Landers: I am not a hippie or a far-out creep with long hair and sandals. I attend a good Eastern school and am a law-abiding, peace-loving citizen. I want to ask a serious question and I need a direct answer. Is marihuana dangerous? Many of my friends smoke pot and have advanced some good arguments in favor of it. They claim pot gives them a high feeling but no hangover like alcohol. They insist it is not physically addictive and a person can quit without experiencing withdrawal symptoms. No one I know who smokes pot will admit to taking anything stronger. This discounts the theory that pot smokers often go on to other stuff. They say the only thing wrong with pot is that it is illegal, and the law will soon be changed. I have never used pot, but I confess the idea is somewhat appealing. Perhaps your answer will help me decide. It may also be useful for some of my pot-smoking friends, including my fiancée.—*Undecided*

Dear Undecided: My answer to your question, "Is pot dangerous?" would cut no mustard. You might as well, ask your mother. An answer from three of the country's most distinguished psychiatrists, however, might make a dent.

Dr. Edward M. Litin, head of psychiatry at Mayo Clinic, Rochester, Minnesota, says: "I am dead set against marihuana because it produces confusion, hallucinations, and impulsive behavior. While some marihuana users have no inclination to try anything stronger, many *do* graduate from pot to more powerful drugs, and of course this can lead to serious trouble."

Dr. Zigmond M. Lebensohn, chief of psychiatry at Sibley Memorial Hospital, Washington, says: "I consider marihuana a serious problem for our 'alienated youth.' It is *not* harmless, as some users insist, and I am sorry the notion that it is nonaddictive has gained such wide acceptance. Although people who use marihuana do not experience withdrawal symptoms when it is removed, they are tremendously drawn to it and many users go back to marihuana after they have left the hospital because they want to recapture the pleasurable feeling. This dependency is just as serious as a physical addiction. In my professional experience I have seen a number of young people experience psychotic episodes precipitated by marihuana. Intense emotional experiences were sufficient to trip the balance in the direction of acute psychotic disorganization. This sometimes lasts for weeks and even months. In certain instances, the effects continue indefinitely and cause complete disruption of a life plan, tremendous expense to the smoker and his family, and the end is often a totally unproductive human being. Some individuals have been able to use marihuana and get away with it, but these individuals have stable nervous systems. Most young people who smoke marihuana do not have stable central nervous systems, and for this reason it is particularly dangerous for them."

Dr. Phillip Solomon, clinical professor of psychiatry at Harvard, says: "Some people have smoked marihuana for years and have experienced no damage whatever. For others it has proved disastrous. Marihuana is not harmless. It may not be addictive but it *is* habit-forming. In unstable personalities, marihuana can be the trigger that precipitates psychosis. Marihuana is the coward's approach to dealing with life's problems. Escaping does not produce a solution. It merely distorts the judgment and delays acting on a solution. Prolonged and continued escape can and will create serious incapacitation and move a person farther and farther from reality."

So, there you have it from three leading authorities. I don't expect you to listen to me, but I do hope you listen to them.

Dear Ann Landers: I have a friend who is fat as cow. She says she loves to eat more than anything in the world and she will not give up this pleasure. She also would like to have a nice figure, which is very hard to do considering that she is constantly stuffing herself with candy, cake, cookies, caramel corn, and everything fattening you can think of. Last week my friend told me she has hit on a system that will allow her to eat whatever she pleases and not put on weight. She packs in the rich food and then she goes to the bathroom and forces herself to throw up. She claims if the food is not in her it will not make her gain weight. Is this true or false?—*The Asker*

Dear Asker: It is false, foolish, and dangerous. When your friend throws up the food, she also loses the gastric juices which are essential to good health. The girl sounds cuckoo to me and I hope she will see a doctor and get on a sensible diet before she wrecks her health.

Dear Ann Landers: How come you fell for that crazy letter from the woman who said she loved her husband but she had to divorce him because he gave her asthma and hives? Any idiot knows it's not possible to catch asthma or hives. These illnesses are not contagious. Now if she got the measles or the flu from her husband, that would be another matter. I hope you will correct yourself in the paper because a lot of people accept your word and you owe the public sensible answers.—*Disillusioned*

Dear Dis: A person does not catch asthma or hives from another person in the same way that he might catch the mumps, but any physician will tell you that hives and asthma can be psychogenerated, which in plain English means "caused by an emotional problem." Fear, resentment, conflict, and guilt can make a person so ill he is unable to get out of bed in the morning. Ulcers, headaches, and backaches are only a few of the ailments that are often traced to an emotional problem. No one would be so foolish as to say an ulcer is contagious, but almost everybody who has an ulcer got it from somebody, usually a relative or a business associate.

Dear Ann Landers: A friend of mine who is normally quiet—in fact, you might even say depressed—showed up at a party last week in very high spirits. I couldn't get over the change in her personality so I pulled her aside and asked what had come over her. She swore me to secrecy, took a pillbox out of her purse and showed me some capsules which she said had done wonders for her. I asked what was in the capsules, and she said she didn't know and didn't care. When I asked the name of the doctor who had recommended them she replied, "I got these from my cleaning woman. I wouldn't say a word to my doctor because he might not approve and I'd be down in the dumps again." I have never been one to take medicine. In fact, I'm one of those people who has to be dying before I will take an aspirin. I admit I am tempted to try these capsules just to see what they would do to me. Do you know anything about this sort of pepper-upper?—*Need A Boost*

Dear Need: No more than you do—which is nothing. But this I *do* know: Any woman who would let her cleaning lady prescribe medication has a loose connection in her attic. If you need a boost, go to your doctor. Perhaps you aren't getting enough rest. Maybe your blood pressure is low or you need more sugar or a thyroid check. A physician should decide. People who get pepped up with capsules pay for it later. It's like racing a motor at top speed. It could shake you apart. The magic medicine that puts a tiger in your tank could cause sleeplessness, severe heart palpitations, melancholia—or worse.

Dear Ann Landers: Dentists are, in my opinion, the most backward of all professionals. If Benjamin Franklin had not invented false teeth, people would be walking around toothless today. I have been reading articles on tooth transplants since I was a child. Dentists have been "experimenting" for twenty years. I have written to the authors of the articles to learn which dentists perform the procedure. The replies were vague. I never did find a dentist who could transplant a tooth. All they know is drilling and pulling and dentures and partial plates. They are too busy raking in the money to learn anything new. Today when kidneys, liver, human hair, and even the heart can be transplanted, is it too much to ask that the dentists get busy and join the twentieth century?—*Exposed Nerve*

Dear Nerve: There are hundreds of dentists who transplant teeth. Where have you been looking? Transplanting teeth began in the eighteenth century. Your reference to Benjamin Franklin is interesting. The agony produced by his handmade teeth (fashioned out of hippopotamus ivory, wood, gold plate, rivets, screws, human incisor teeth, and steel springs) started dentists experimenting with tooth transplants. Tooth donors, principally poor people, were secured through newspaper ads. A New York paper in 1772 carried the following notice: "Teeth—any person willing to dispose of his front teeth apply to Number 28 Maiden Lane. A generous price will be given. N.B.: Four guineas [about $40 in today's currency] will be paid for every tooth." The practice of transplantation was ultimately abandoned for several reasons. First, it failed to meet the needs of the masses. Second, many diseases were transmitted from donor to recipient (most notably syphilis). Third, the medical world learned of the rejection phenomenon. After a few months, transplanted teeth loosened and fell out. A hundred years later, however, dentists began experimenting once again with transplanted teeth, and the techniques have been vastly improved. Today, a transplanted tooth will last four or five years. The knowledge gained by dentists in their transplant procedures has helped lay the theoretical groundwork which made possible the kidney and liver transplants, and now the heart. Now, aren't you ashamed?

Five

M.Y.O.B.

If all the world's meddlers were laid end to end, they'd be a lot more comfortable. And so would everyone else.

It is difficult to evaluate the destruction wrought by "well-meaning" relatives, "deeply concerned" friends, and "interested" neighbors who feel it is their "duty" to "say something." Over the years I have advised so many people to "mind your own business" that the phrase became tiresome even to my ears, so I reduced it to M Y.O.B.

Prying is an extremely popular sport. It is free, provides diversion, and can be easily disguised as "friendly concern." I never cease to marvel at the number of reasonably intelligent people who will relate the most intimate details of their personal lives merely because some clod has the gall to ask questions which are clearly none of his business.

A bewildered bride once asked what to do about an obnoxious aunt who, whenever they met, patted her stomach solicitously and inquired, "Anything in the oven yet?" I told the bewildered bride to respond in this manner: "I'll forgive you for asking that question if you'll forgive me for not answering it."

The best rule to follow is this: Was I asked for my opinion? Is it really wanted? Does the situation affect my life in an important way? If you get a No answer to any of these questions, then M.Y.O.B.

It demands maturity and discipline to remain silent when someone we care about seems headed down a collision course. Particularly is it difficult when we feel it might be possible to save a worthy person from heartbreak and disaster. But advice must be sought, it must not be inflicted. And this is the crucial hook on which your decision should hang.

A great deal is being said and written these days about human rights. The Constitution guarantees all United States citizens freedom of speech, freedom of worship, and the right to peaceful assembly to petition the government for redress of grievances. One of the most sacred rights of every human being, however, is not mentioned in the Constitution, or anywhere else, for that matter. It is the right to be left alone.

Dear Ann Landers: No wonder people think you're wonderful. You conveniently look the other way while they raise hell. You and your "M.Y.O.B." philosophy are partly responsible for the decline in American morals. I'm a landlady who doesn't stand for any kitchey-cooing on my premises. I own two buildings, and my caretakers have orders to tell me if any female tenant has male guests who leave after 1 A.M. You know very well, Ann Landers, that a single girl who entertains men after midnight is not playing Scrabble. It's not enough that people pay their rent and don't rip out the plumbing. I expect decent morals, and if they don't measure up they can live somewhere else.—*Aunt Nettie From Wilkes-Barre*

I told Aunt Nettie that by the time a girl is old enough to rent an apartment she has decided what kind of games she wants to play. And I added, of course, "M.Y.O.B., Auntie."

Dear Ann Landers: Martha and I have been friends for years. She told me she was sorry she was unable to work with me on a church project because she was going to the hospital next week for "a little surgery." When I asked her what kind of surgery, she cut me dead with one word—"minor." I felt as if I had been slapped across the face. I thought about it all the next day and decided to telephone her physician in the hope that he would tell me it was nothing serious. Well, Ann, I've never been so hurt in my life. The doctor told me to mind my own business and that under no circumstances would he discuss a patient's condition with a third party. I think he hung up on me. Why would a person be ashamed of having an operation? And why was the doctor so rude when I was merely inquiring about the welfare of a friend?—*Chopped Down*

Dear Chopped: If Martha had wanted to give you any information about her surgery, she would have volunteered it. The doctor gave you good advice. Take it.

Dear Ann Landers: I have a strong suspicion there's a little hanky-panky going on in our church choir. The choirmaster is a married man, thirty-two years of age. He has been writing special arrangements for an alto whose voice is embarrassingly unimpressive. This alto is a divorced woman who is at least five years older than the choirmaster. They don't go anywhere together publicly, but I have seen his car parked outside her home on three occasions. She looks at him with cow eyes when she sings her solos and it is sickening. What do you think about such monkeyshines in a church group? Should I speak to the clergyman?—*A Moral Person*

Moral Person received one of the shortest replies on record: *Dear M.P.:* M.Y.O.B.

Dear Ann Landers: Eight of us girls get together every two weeks to play cards. One of the girls who has been married three years announced in April she was expecting a baby on October 12. Well, on August 18 she gave birth. Her child weighed nine pounds and eight ounces and had a full head of hair. She made a point of explaining that the baby was premature. Please tell us how in the world a premature baby can weigh more than most nine-month babies? When we told her she must have miscalculated the date of birth, she stubbornly insisted that she did no such thing. Since this woman is so obstinate we decided to ask you to check out the facts and settle the argument.—*Seven Disbelievers*

Dear Seven: What baffles me is not the size of the child, but the size of your interest. You girls need something to do in your spare time. The Salvation Army needs volunteers.

Dear Ann Landers: Our daughter who is a junior in college is interested in Sid, a young graduate student. Last week he was a guest in our house. Sid shared a bedroom with our thirteen-year-old son. This morning after our daughter and Sid left for school our son told us he had an opportunity to learn a few things. Sid's suitcase had someone else's initials on it. His driver's license indicated that he is twenty-three, not twenty-four. He owes someone $200 according to a note in his wallet. There was a mushy letter in his suitcase from a girl who lives in Buffalo. Also, he carries a picture in his wallet of *two* girls—our daughter and another girl. What do you make of this?—*Concerned Parents*

Dear Parents: You have a right to be *deeply* concerned—about that little punk you're raising. Teach the kid to mind his own business.

Dear Ann Landers: Please tell me how to deal with a neighbor who asks personal questions in such an innocent way that she disarms me completely? Here are some samples of her wide-eyed inquiries: Are you pregnant? How much income tax did your husband pay this year? How much did your draperies cost? Was that a wig you wore the other night? Sometimes I blurt out the answer because I can't think fast enough. Later I could kick myself. I am no match for her. Help!—*Inadequate*

Dear In: The next reader has the answer you've been needing.

Dear Ann: I was once a shy violet who felt an obligation to answer every question put to me. I have since learned that the person who has the poor taste or the pure gall to ask questions which are clearly none of his business needs to be put in his place. When a neighbor asks, "When are you going to have another baby?" or "How much did your living room carpeting cost?" I clobber her with this one-liner: "Why would you ask such a personal question?" It never fails to squelch the nerviest and the nosiest.—*New Me*

Dear New: Thanks on behalf of the meek. Although the Bible says they shall inherit the earth, it's nice to have a little protection until the inheritance comes through.

Dear Ann Landers: What on earth is wrong with a mother who follows her four-year-old son around on the playground with a comb and brush and damp washcloth? This woman is very intelligent when it comes to literature and music, but when it comes to raising children she is a moron. Yesterday her son fell in the mud, and she scolded him for getting dirty. The woman made such a fuss I felt sorry for the child. I finally couldn't keep quiet any longer so I told her that all kids get dirty and no kid ever died from it. She told me to mind my own business. What do *you* say?— *Trying To Help*

Dear Trying: I say all kids get dirty and no kid ever died from it. But mind your own business.

Dear Ann Landers: My husband and I have been married five years. We have two children and I am expecting a third baby in February. We want six children and hope to have our family complete by the time we celebrate our tenth wedding anniversary. My husband is in the middle income group and we never expect to be rich. The problem is relatives on both sides. When they heard I was pregnant again, their comments were insulting. My mother-in-law thinks it is "just terrible." My own father said something is wrong with people who "multiply like rabbits." My sister told us we remind her of the slum dwellers she used to visit as a social worker. Please tell us how to let them know we *want* a large family and to mind their own business.— *Happy*

Dear Happy: I can't improve on your wording. It was perfect.

Dear Ann Landers: My sister's husband died three years ago. Sally went into a depression, and the doctor suggested she go to work and get her mind off herself. (She has no children.) At work, Sally met a married man whose wife is in a mental hospital. They fell madly in love. She is ruining the family name because of her shameless behavior. She goes everywhere with this man, even to church. I love my sister and I want her to have a respectable life. I've talked to her until I am blue in the face, but she tells me she cannot give him up and he needs her as much as she needs him. Shall I go to the man and tell him he is married and to leave my sister alone?—*Interested Yvonne*

Dear Yvonne: It isn't necessary for you to tell the man he is married. He knows. it. Why don't you mind your own business?

Dear Ann Landers: Am I justified in being upset with my mother or am I being "adolescent"? I am seventeen and have been going with a wonderful fellow who is taking summer courses at a university. Ron has written some poems just for me. They are the most sensitive and exquisite words I have ever read. I learned this afternoon that my mother read several of Ron's poems at her Ladies Aid when they met at our home last week. When I told Mother I was shocked, she said, "I thought the poems were so beautiful I wanted the ladies to hear them. Beautiful things belong to the world." I am disappointed, angry, and resentful. Comment please—*J.*

Dear J.: The poetry was written for you and not for the world, or the Ladies Aid. I wonder if your mother knows what M.Y.O.B. means?

Dear Ann Landers: I've been going with a lovely young widow for about eighteen months. Sara lives in another city, but we see each other every weekend. We are in love and plan to be married. Sara told me early in our friendship that her husband killed himself. Somehow my mother and sisters learned about the suicide, and they are trying to talk me out of marrying her. They say when a married man kills himself it means his wife failed him. Sara is sensitive and insecure; her life has been a trying and lonely one. I believe it is unfair to say she failed her husband, and I resent the suggestion that she is a poor marriage risk. I'd like your views.—*Color Me Blue*

Dear Blue: First, about your family: Color them vicious. Suicide is an irrational act. A husband or a wife who has lived through the nightmare should be spared the burden of guilt. If you love the woman and want to marry her, disregard your family's cruel insinuations. And you might tell them to M.Y.O.B.

Dear Ann: Our twenty-year-old daughter is about to be married. She has a well-paying job but has always spent more money than she made. I know this girl has a staggering number of unpaid bills for clothes, records, costume jewelry, luggage—anything she could buy on credit. I have asked her four times if her bills are paid, but she lies better than most people tell the truth. Yes, Ann, I've failed, but it's too late to do anything about that now. What I need to know is should I tell her fiancé that his bride-to-be is in debt up to her neck? Rush the advice.—*Too Late Smart.*

Dear Too Late: M.Y.O.B., Mother, but urge your daughter to tell him. If she springs unpaid bills on a brand-new husband it could get things off to a wobbly start.

Dear Ann Landers: I am a widow over sixty. My son is a bachelor thirty-two years old. Hal has traveled and worked abroad, is successful in business, and has had his own apartment off and on. When my husband died two years ago Hal decided to give up his apartment and move in with me. Friends and relatives have made snide remarks, hinting that something must be wrong with a thirty-two-year-old man who lives with his mother. Hal says he enjoys it here, and frankly it's wonderful for me. Hal is not interested in any specific woman at this time but he has had some serious affairs with women, so there is nothing wrong with him in *that* direction. Am I doing him an injustice by allowing him to live here?—*R.X.L.*

Dear R.X.L.: If a son enjoys living in his mother's home and if she enjoys having him there, whose business is it? It's nobody's business, and your relatives should be told as much.

Dear Ann Landers: Keith and I haven't been married very long, three months to be exact. Something is bothering me, and I'm afraid it will bother me until we get it talked out. Keith went with a girl for two years before he started to go with me. I had seen the girl three or four times, but I never got to know her. Now that Keith and I are man and wife I think he should tell me how far they went and exactly why they broke up. I didn't ask him these questions while we were going together because I figured it was none of my business. But now that we are married I think everything that has to do with Keith is my business. Am I right? —*Nothing Withheld*

Dear Nothing: No, you are wrong. What happened between Keith and the girl wasn't your business *then* and it's not your business *now*. I admire him for keeping his trap shut.

Dear Ann Landers: My husband is a photo nut. He spends hundreds of dollars on equipment, chemicals, paper, film, and so on. His photos are terrific. My beef is this: At every family gathering he shoots dozens of pictures. Then he slaves for hours making prints. The relatives can well afford to pay fifty cents apiece for these wonderful 5 x 7 and 8 x 10 pictures. But my hardheaded husband says, "No, I wouldn't think of charging them. I do this for fun." Fun, my eye. He does it with money that could be better spent buying nicer clothing for his family or fixing up our house. Why should he be so balky about asking relatives to pay for prints? I think he is a sucker. What do you think?—*Hypo Harriet, The Lenshound's Wife*

Dear Wife: The lens-hound sounds like a sweet guy who enjoys his hobby. If he sold his pictures it would no longer be a hobby—it would be a business. So why don't you keep your nose out of his hydroquinone?

Dear Ann: How can I save my forty-eight-year-old brother from making a darn fool of himself? Artie never married. He has been like a second father to our children. They love to have him around, and so do we. He is witty, generous, and a great human being. The problem is this: Artie has been bald for as long as I can remember. Well, last night he came over and we almost fell dead. Artie took off his hat and proudly displayed a head of golden curls. The hairpiece looks surprisingly genuine, but it's just not our Artie. I'm afraid he'll be the laughingstock of the town if he insists on wearing that thing. Is this second childhood or what? He said he feels like a collge kid again. We need an outsider to advise us.—*D.C.*

Dear D.C.: It's Artie's head, and if he wants to put a rug on it, why should it bother you? It's how *he* feels that counts, and apparently he feels pretty good. So M.Y.O.B.

Dear Ann Landers: I am a seventeen-year-old girl who has a mother problem. She doesn't think any of the boys I like are good enough for me. This one is too short and that one lives in the wrong part of town. For the fourth time in two months mother has arranged a date for me with the son or the nephew of her bridge-club ladies. These fellows are jerky and I can't stand them. I've told her how I feel but she says I'm too young to know my own mind. What burns me up is that she doesn't even *ask* me. She makes the date and I have to go. Is this right or wrong?—*Like For Sale*

Dear Like: A pushy mother often spoils the chances of a very nice guy by cramming him down a daughter's throat. Maybe your mom needs something to keep her occupied, like some business of her own to mind.

Dear Ann Landers: We are writing about a relative who is sixty-six years old. (I will call him Uncle D.) His wife died four months ago. She was a fine woman but very strict with him. Uncle D. has been spending a lot of time (and money) on a young girl who is a gold digger and a tramp. She is forty years younger than he is, and you son't have to be a genius to figure this one out. I decided to have a talk with Uncle D. and point out a few things that he might not be aware of. His answer was, "I know what I'm doing. This girl could be my bluebird of happiness." What should we do?—*Hate To See It Happen*

Dear Happen: Nothing. If Uncle D. marries a girl young enough to be his granddaughter, the only part of that bluebird he will see is the bill. M.Y.O.B.

Dear Ann Landers: I am a mother who paid a high price for her snoopiness. I was determined that my teen-ager, Lucille, would never put anything over on me. I read her diary, looked through her bureau drawers, her purse, and her pockets. I eavesdropped on her telephone conversations and did everything imaginable to keep tabs on her. The results were tragic. Lucille became an extraordinary liar. That girl could think up things that would baffle the FBI. Our relationship deteriorated into a bitter contest—Lucille striving to see how much she could get away with and me figuring out ways to trap her. Finally she wound up in serious trouble. I learned too late that trust and confidence are more effective tools for building honesty than suspicion and investigation. I should have minded my own business.—*Sorry Now*

Dear Sorry: You said it and I thank you.

Dear Ann Landers: You seem to have it in for mothers-in-law. I'll bet anything yours is a pain in the neck. My only son married a little nothing. She is plain looking, has no style, no family background, no taste, can't cook, can't bake, her house is a mess. Yesterday I could stand it no longer so I said. "Lucille, dear, is there a reason for leaving that filthy dishrag in the sink?" She replied icily, "If it doesn't bother me why should it bother you?" One thing led to another and finally she said, "I resent your interfering in my life and I wish you would stop it." After all, Ann, I turned my son over to this girl, and I want her to do right by him. Was I wrong?—*Just His Mother*

Dear His Mother: Yes. It's her home, her sink, and her dishrag, and you should not have said anything. As for my mother-in-law being a pain in the neck, you're mistaken. She's a gem. Twenty-nine years and never has she offered even one suggestion. Why don't you take a lesson from my mother-in-law?

Dear Ann Landers: My husband and I are in our late twenties. We've been married seven years, have a lovely home, excellent jobs, and are content. For reasons which we do not wish to discuss with anyone, we have no children. Our friends all have children, and they badger us mercilessly because we have none. They insist something must be drastically wrong with us—that we are selfish and shortsighted. The stock phrase is "You don't know what you're missing." They also say we will no doubt end up in the divorce court because a marriage without children is sure to fail. Why don't people leave us alone? Please, Ann, print this letter and inform the meddlers that all couples without children are not miserable.—*Irate*

Dear Irate: Childless couples owe neither apology nor explanation to outsiders. When the subject comes up, say, "We've beat the topic into the ground, now let's talk about something else."

While there is a great deal to be said for having a family, there is something to be said for not having a family—if you don't want one. The following letter presents an interesting point of view.

Dear Ann Landers: I'm bored with all that stuff and nonsense in your column about the glories of parenthood. You won't print this letter because it slaughters a sacred cow, but some couples, believe it or not, don't want children and we are among them. My husband and I have enjoyed forty grand years together. The notion that children are a comfort to parents in their sunset years is horse feathers. We have many friends who are in financial straitjackets because of their children. My sister and her husband were never able to go to Europe or buy a new car because their children have been on their backs all their lives. My brother's wife passed away last October, and their four children have been fighting ever since about who should take the old man in. The truth is, nobody wants him. Whenever we spend an evening with our relatives, we go home and congratulate each other.—*Just Us And Glad Of It*

Dear Just: Apparently the decision to remain childless was right—for you. But not everyone's kids are like your nieces and nephews. Some children are considerate, self-supporting, self-sufficient, and self-respecting—because their parents raised them that way.

Dear Ann Landers: Is it a private battle or can anyone get in on it? May I add my two cents' worth to the "childless couple argument"? There is nothing sadder than a couple without children. It's heartbreaking to see them stretched out, relaxing around the swimming pool, suntanned and miserable, trotting off to Europe like lonesome fools. What an empty life! Nothing but money to spend and time to enjoy it! They miss all the fun of doing without "for the children's sake." How selfish they become, buying what they want and doing as they please.

Everyone should have children. No one should be allowed to escape the rewarding experiences that accompany every stage of parenthood. Those all-night vigils, the coughing spells, drunken baby-sitters, saturated mattresses, midnight rushes to the hospital, separating little brothers and sisters when they try to kill each other. I pity the couple without children to brighten the cocktail hour. The little darlings have a way of brushing a martini from your hand and massaging the potato chips into the rugs. And what fun when they fight you for the olive! The scuffles in the presence of guests make for a lot of laughs—and an early breakdown. The *real* satisfactions come later.

Those thoughtful discussions when the report card reveals your prodigy is one step below a nitwit. Then the hours of arguing. You try to pin it on *his* side of the family. He tries to pin it on *your* side of the family. But children are worth it all. The warm feeling the first time you take the boy hunting. He didn't mean to shoot you in the leg. Remember how he cried? He was so disappointed that you weren't a deer. The limp is with you to this day. Nothing builds character like practicing self-control. And what better practice than watching the warm smile of a lad with the sun glittering on $500 worth of dental braces—ruined by peanut brittle.

The childless couple lives in a vacuum. They try to fill the lonesome hours with golf, bridge, trips, civic affairs. Sometimes the tranquillity and extra money are enough to drive a person crazy! All you have to do is look at these empty, unfulfilled shells to see what the years have done to them. He looks boyish, unlined, rested. She is slim, well-groomed, and youthful. It isn't natural. If they had kids like the rest of us they'd be beat-up, gray, wrinkled, and nervous wrecks, too.

So, Ann Landers, when people ask childless couples why they don't have a family, I hope you will remember this letter and add for good measure, "Mind your own business."—*San Francisco*

Six

MANNERS AND MORALS

Often a reader will tell me he feels ashamed and worthless because he has done something "immoral." In a great many instances, he has done nothing immoral; he has simply displayed bad manners. In some cases, a tortured soul will write and want to know if what he has done was a sin or "just not proper." Often, it is neither.

The best test for morality is to ask yourself, "Is it good manners?" This might sound absurd, but it is a true criterion. Every immoral act contains an element of bad manners since it disregards the rights and feelings of others.

Jonathan Swift said it best: "Good manners is the art of making people comfortable. Whoever makes the fewest persons uneasy is the best bred in the company." To this I would like to add—he is also the most moral.

———————

Dear Ann Landers: I am a homemaker, aged thirty, and have a good husband and three fine children. We are upper-middle-class folks who live in an upper-middle-class neighborhood and have upper-middle-class friends. When I'm in the house alone in the morning, after the children go off to school and my husband leaves for work, I like to do my housework with no clothes on. Yes, you read correctly—with no clothes on. I pull the shades and draw the draperies. No one can possibly see me. Last week I confided this to a friend and she said I must be off my rocker—that there is something immoral or sick, or both, about a person who would walk around the house nude. I don't know why I do it; all I know is I enjoy it. Is it bad manners? Is it immoral?—*Lady Godiva*

Dear Lady: I can only guess that you enjoy doing your housework with no clothes on because you like the feeling of total freedom, as some swimmers do. Maybe you enjoy the sheer nonconformity of doing your housework in the nude. If you wish to walk around in your own home naked as a jaybird or wearing a raccoon coat, whose business is it? It may be unorthodox, but that doesn't mean it is either immoral or bad manners.

Dear Ann Landers: I could kiss you for printing that letter from Lady Godiva, the woman who enjoys doing her housework in the nude. For years, I thought maybe I was a freak because I do the same thing. Naturally, I've never breathed my secret to a soul—not even my husband. I was greatly relieved when you said it was neither immoral nor sick, and that so long as she kept her shades down it was nobody's business. I'm a woman in my forties who also enjoys the freedom of doing her housework in the nude. I can bend and stretch, unencumbered. Now I zip right through this eight-room house in less than two hours.—*Another Jaybird*

A staggering number of housewives wrote to confide that they, too, enjoy doing their housework in the nude. Here's another jaybird from Memphis:

Dear Ann: Tell Lady Godiva she's not crazy and she's not alone. I've been doing my housework in my birthday suit for twenty years. I consider myself normal and intelligent. As a bride I was forever sewing torn seams and restitching pockets which had caught on knobs. One day I took off my housedress when I got soaked to the skin (a frying pan plopped into the dishwater). I so enjoyed the feeling of freedom that I've been cleaning house in the nude ever since. I can report only one minor mishap. Several months ago while ironing a bed sheet, I stood a little too close to the board and burned my stomach. Nothing serious— just painful. Please warn the girls—*Me, In The Flesh*

Dear You: Sorry about your stomach. Take note, Jaybirds. Other hazards of prancing about unclothed are in the next letter from Louisville.

Dear Ann Landers: I used to do my housework in the nude, but a recent experience cured me. Our minister expressed the wish to see our new baby. The time set for his visit was 2 P.M. I was fresh out of coffee cream and phoned my neighbor to ask if she'd bring over half a bottle. I grabbed a face towel to wrap around my middle so I could reach out for the coffee cream. I opened the door quickly and shouted, "Boy, am I glad to see you, Honey!" To my everlasting shame, it was the minister. He was so startled, his glasses almost fell off. He mumbled, "I'll be back next week when I can bring my wife." I slammed the door shut and just sat there and shook for twenty minutes. To this day, I'm unable to look him in the face. (P.S. You can be sure I'm no longer a nudist.)—*Still Blushing*

Dear Blushing: The next letter from Kansas City may be a comfort.

Dear Ann: I wonder if Lady Godiva saw the news item in the paper about an Ohio housewife. She was doing her laundry in the basement and impulsively decided to take off the soiled housedress she was wearing and throw it into the machine. Her hair had just been set in pincurls and the pipes overhead were leaking. She spotted her son's football helmet and put it on her head. There she was, stark naked (except for the football helmet) when she heard a cough. The woman turned around and found herself staring into the face of the meter-reader from the gas and electric company. As he headed for the door, his only comment was, "I hope your team wins, lady."

Dear Ann Landers: I'm a girl sixteen years old and a junior in high school. I have one date a week, usually on Saturday night. Sometimes I go out on Friday night, too, if it's something special. My mother has decided I must fill out a date-form. She wants me to answer about twenty questions. Here are some examples: 1. Name of your date, his age, and his address. 2. Occupation of his father. 3. Where did you go? 4. How much money did he spend? 5. Did he try to kiss you? 6. Did you let him? 7. Do you think he will ever amount to anything? 8. Would you like your children to look like him? I think these questions are dumb. Will you please tell me if I am a rebellious and headstrong teen-ager, as my mother says, or do I have a right to be bugged?—*Insulted*

Dear Insulted: Your mother should know the name of every fellow you date because you should have introduced each one. She also should know where you are going. But the other questions, particularly No. 8, are indeed dumb, and I don't blame you for being resentful.

Dear Ann Landers: My dad used to have a great build in his younger days. But a lot of beer has gone down the hatch since then and now he's sort of fat. Dad insists on sitting around in the house in swimming trunks. When my friends come over I'm embarrassed. My mother doesn't like it either. Every now and then she'll say, "Harold, go put on a robe." But he pays no attention. My dad is wonderful and I love all 220 pounds of him, but do you think he should sit in the living room in swimming trunks when I have company?—*Gandhi's Daughter*

Dear Daughter: When your mother gives out with "Harold, go put on a robe," Harold should go put on a robe. You wouldn't sit in the living room in *your* bathing suit when Dad entertains business friends, would you? Point this out to him. It might help.

Dear Ann Landers: I've always had a private telephone line until recently. Now I'm on a party line— the other party is the family next door. They have a seventeen-year-old son who screams, "Hey, get off the line!" whenever I pick up the receiver. What possible interest could I have in listening to this boy jabber with his high-school friends? After being shouted at and insulted several times, I wrote a letter to the boy's father. I received no reply. If someone had written a similar letter to me, I would have gone over immediately to discuss the problem. Now whenever I encounter a member of that family, they turn their heads. Do you feel I should not have written the letter?—*Grand Rapids*

Dear Grand: It would have been better to discuss the matter in person, but the father should have responded to your letter as a matter of courtesy. Parents do their children no favor when they take their side against adults who have legitimate complaints. This boy was clearly disrespectful. In most cities, the telephone company will change your party line partner if you have a good reason for requesting it. And you have.

Dear Ann Landers: Last night my husband gave me notice. He said, "I refuse to go to any more parties. I am sick of spending time with people we don't care about—so we can be part of a phony social set. I would prefer to stay at home and read." Frankly, so would I. Entertaining has gotten out of hand. Every hostess I know just about kills herself trying to do something different and impressive. Our own guest list is loaded with bores to whom we are indebted simply because we have accepted their invitations. But how does a person withdraw from the mad whirl of entertaining? Once you're in it, you're in it, unless you go broke and can't afford to keep up. I need help and I need it now. Is there a door?—*Lake Forest*

Dear Lake Forest: You'll have no problem finding the door once you've decided you want to get out. Univac would have a tough time totaling the hours of wasted energy spent entertaining meaningless acquaintances in the United States suburbs alone. The way to get out of the rat race is simple. Quit running. Don't accept invitations from bores. And don't extend any.

Dear Ann Landers: The letter from Well-Mannered Girl, who was disgusted with her parents because they talked with food in their mouths, might have been written by me when I was thirteen. I, too, was a brash and arrogant girl who looked down on my foreign-born parents because their table manners weren't very elegant and they didn't speak like the parents of my friends. My mother and father are both gone now, and I realize they were remarkable people. Perhaps they lacked polish and refinement, but they had compassion and integrity and a gift for laughter. People who feel that Mom and Dad aren't quite up to their fancy standards need to look beyond the superficial trappings. Their values are clearly out of joint. Children should love their parents for their fine qualities and let them know it before it is—*Too Late*.

Dear Too Late: There's a special lesson to be learned from your letter. I hope it is read and reread by millions of teenagers all over the land.

Dear Ann Landers: I'm an ardent club worker who spends a great deal of time on the telephone. I can't stand it when women eat while they are talking. That crunching sound over the phone drives me bonkers. The other evening one woman was making so much noise I asked, "How is the celery?" She replied, "I'm not eating celery. It's potato chips." And she continued to crunch. Another woman who tipples frequently speaks with an ice cube in her mouth. This morning she said, "Just a minute. I have to stir this drink." Then I heard the tinkling and the gulping. Am I getting crotchety in my old age, or is it rude to eat and drink while on the phone?—*Fuss-Budget*

Dear Fuss: People who munch, crunch, and gulp on the phone are impolite. If it annoys you, speak up, woman.

Dear Ann Landers: My boyfriend was over last night, and we were sitting on the sofa watching TV. My earring fell off and rolled under the piano. I asked him to please move the piano and get it for me. He said, "It's less dangerous, physically, for a woman to move a piano than for a man." For your information, Ann, he is a 180-pound construction worker and in perfect physical condition. I told him I didn't think his attitude was gentlemanly. He claims any doctor will tell you that women have stronger constitutions than men and they live longer. He told me to move the piano myself. What do you have to say about this, Ann Landers?—*Myrtle*

Dear Myrtle: Ask your boyfriend if he has ever seen a lady piano-mover.

Dear Ann Landers: Am I bighearted, or do I have the word "sucker" written all over my face? There are eleven houses on this block, but anybody who wants to borrow a cup of sugar or an aspirin rings my bell. The lady next door is married to a man who can buy and sell my husband ten times, yet she has been using my washing machine for three weeks. The man across the street had trouble getting his car started. Of all the places he could have gone for help, he picked me. (Yes, I'm a strong woman, but wouldn't you have thought he'd have asked a man to help him?) I pushed this nut's car every day for two weeks. Yesterday I said, "Look, I'm pushing you for the last time. Get a new battery and leave me alone." Now he is mad. Am I an oddball? I don't ask my neighbors for the time of the day. Please give me some advice.—*The Magnet*

Dear Mag: There's a vast difference between lending a neighbor an aspirin and pushing a man's car every day for two weeks. If *you* don't know the difference, then you *are* an oddball.

Dear Ann Landers: My dear husband passed away three months ago. He was sixty-eight years old. Typical of his generous nature, he was more concerned for me than for himself. When he learned his days were numbered, he made me promise I would ask his widowed sister, Kate, to live with me. His last words were, "I will rest in peace only if I know you are not alone." Well, Ann, I knew Kate took a little sherry before supper, but I didn't know she also drank gin in the morning. I was shocked to discover she drinks all day, which explains why she falls down and injures herself so often. Kate is very heavy and has a hard time getting around even when she's sober. It's easier for me to bring her meals on a tray than to get her up and dressed. Ever since she moved in I've been on twenty-four-hour duty, and I'm exhausted. I realize Kate is a sick woman who needs care, but she is ruining my health. Would I be dishonoring my husband's memory if I asked her to leave?—*D.G.D.*

Dear D.G.D.: No, on the contrary, had your husband known the truth he would not have made such a request. Surely it was not his wish that you spend your remaining years playing nursemaid to an alcoholic. Ask Kate's physician to suggest a hospital—preferably an A.A. type, if he can persuade her.

Dear Ann Landers: My husband passed away five months ago. This may sound terrible, but his death freed me from a living hell. We never had any children because he didn't want any. For eleven years I put up with his lying, drinking, gambling, and abusive language. On three separate occasions he brought women home to spend the night. I was quietly making plans to leave him when he was killed in an accident. A long-time friend who lost his wife two years ago has asked me to marry him. I have said Yes. He is a fine person, and I want to be a mother to his two little girls. Now —the trouble. I asked my clergyman how long it was proper for a widow to wait before she remarries. He said "at least one year." Then I wrote to you. Your reply was, "It's how you feel that counts." Well, Ann, I feel like getting married tomorrow. Who is right, you or the clergyman?—*Dilemma*

Dear Dil: People who go around collecting opinions should be prepared for a variety of answers. The "wait a year" custom is well and good if a widow wishes to pay respect to her deceased husband. But why pay respect to eleven years of hell?

Dear Ann Landers: I see by our newspaper that you firmly believe prolonged mourning is unhealthy. You say it serves no useful purpose and long-time mourning is "self-pity turned inside out." You usually make pretty good sense. I agree in this case that you are right. Now, I would like your views on prolonged courtship. What do you think about couples who go together for years and never seem to get around to marriage? I know of a couple who have been dating for fifteen years. Is this healthy? My initials are the same as yours.—*A.L.*

Dear A.L.: It all depends on the couple. I've said it before and I'll say it again—marriage is not for everyone. Some couples "go together" like salami and rye bread, but they are unable (for a variety of reasons) to function within the framework of marriage. For them marriage is a disaster, and they are better off "going together."

Dear Ann Landers: Last week my oldest brother passed away. Several members of the family came to the funeral from other cities. It was the first time some of them had seen each other in fifteen years. After the funeral, the family gathered at my home. They got drunk, told jokes, sang college songs, and played cards. Some of the younger ones had the radio on in the back of the house and were dancing. About midafternoon seven of them left to go to a movie. I told my sister it was disgraceful, and she said, "You're wrong. I admire them because they aren't hypocrites. Gerald didn't mean anything to them. They hadn't seen him in years. Why pretend?" Something is frightfully wrong with her argument, but what?—*V.I.X.*

Dear V.I.X.: Never mind her argument. Something is frightfully wrong with your relatives. Whether Gerald meant anything to them or not is beside the point. Gerald meant something to *you,* and they were in your home. Jokes, drunkenness, card playing, and dancing are out of place in a house of mourning. They may not be hypocrites, but they are clods.

The following letter sounds like the same family:

Dear Ann Landers: My husband and his brothers were not born with silver spoons in their mouths. It was poker chips. Every year for the past ten, we have gathered in my in-law's home for the major holidays. It's always the same story. No grace is said before meals, and there is no conversation at the table. It's, "Quick, let's eat and get it over with." Then, "Your deal, deuces wild. Ante up. You're shy a blue." This year, we gave up beautiful church services and dinner with my folks so we could drag four small children to look at a deck of cards. I always get a terrific headache from the yelling and the cigar smoke. After an hour of trying to read in the next room and attempting to keep the kids from tearing the house from its foundation, I suggested to my husband that we leave. He said, "I'm in no hurry." My husband agrees that it's smoky and noisy over there, but he also says he enjoys being with his family and that I should be a good sport. Sign me—*Fed Up And Headed For A Showdown.*

Dear Fed: It isn't worth breaking up a home over. Maybe the next letter will make you feel better. More brother-in-law problems—and worse than yours.

Dear Ann Landers: We are people of modest means and could manage on my husband's paycheck if we had only *our* family to take care of. Unfortunately my husband's two brothers are frequently out of work, and they are steady boarders. Last night they were here for dinner. There are five children in our family ranging in age from fourteen to eight. I prepared pork chops and mashed potatoes for supper. I thought thirteen pork chops would be enough to feed us all. Well, I handed the platter to my husband and he took two chops for himself and handed the platter to his brother. His brother took four chops and passed the platter to the other brother who also took four chops. That left three chops for myself and five children. By the time the potatoes got to me there were none left. I said I didn't care for any chops and gave the three older children one chop each. The younger kids and I had cheese sandwiches. I can't tell my husband that I don't want his brothers to come for meals anymore, but no matter how I plan, it is never enough. What can I do?—*Burning*

Dear Burning: Prepare the plates in the kitchen. It is not safe to pass platters to pigs.

Dear Ann Landers: Ever since I married this conceited jackass, it's been the same old story. Whenever we go where there is dance music, he's the first one on the floor. He does a few turns with me, then looks for someone he'd rather dance with. The minute he spots a good-looking girl he grabs her. Her partner, of course, must dance with me. I've tried to explain that some women might prefer the man she has, but he doesn't see that at all. He thinks he's the first choice of every woman in the world. Some of those men who have had beautiful young things snatched out of their arms and got me instead have not been very pleased about it, and I don't blame them. Any suggestions?—*No Trophy Winner*

Dear No Winner: Tell the egomaniac the next time he pulls that stunt you will walk off the dance floor and leave him to fight it out with the man whose partner he is trying to grab. Then do it.

Dear Ann Landers: I'm a widow who is trying to raise a boy alone. Gerald's father died when the boy was six years old. He is now thirteen, and believe me, Ann, I've had my hands full. I am active in our church auxiliary and I hold a state office. I must go to meetings every Tuesday night. There are three very nice young girls in the neighborhood I call on to sit with Gerald. The little redheaded girl is sixteen. The other two girls are fifteen. Last night, Gerald asked me who I had called to sit with him and I told him Gracie. (She is one of the fifteen-year-olds.) He said, "I'd rather have the redhead." This made me stop and consider something that never crossed my mind before. Please read between the lines and tell me what you think.—*Concerned Mother*

Dear Mother: I think when a boy is old enough to ask for a redheaded baby-sitter, he is old enough to stay home alone.

Dear Ann Landers: I came to this rather large city from a small town in Kansas. I was unable to get the kind of employment I had hoped for and my money was running out, so I took a job as a cocktail waitress. The lounge where I work is a favorite hangout for advertising and public relations executives. Their suit sleeves don't have creases like the yokels I used to know back home. (My girl friend told me this is the first thing to look for.) Yesterday, one of the best-looking men I ever saw asked me why a girl with such gorgeous legs was waiting on tables. He said I ought to be a hosiery model and that he could help me. But he doesn't want to talk about the job in his office. He prefers my place. Do you know anything about hosiery modeling? I used to read your column back in Kansas and I trust you, Ann.—*Tough Sledding*

Dear Sledding: That model routine is strictly off the cob. Model agencies have lists a mile long of girls with beautiful gams who are stepping all over each other trying to get jobs. The man's sleeve might not have a crease but I think he's got something up it. Tell him to get lost.

Dear Ann Landers: Should I run an ad in the classified section of this paper? You see, I have a slightly used boyfriend I'd like to get rid of. He broke his leg skiing last November, and I can't get him out of my apartment. The young man is thirty-two, unmarried, handsome in a rugged, Irish way, six feet tall, a superb dancer, doesn't drink or smoke (too much), and he is a writer by profession. This is a part of the problem. He writes checks on our joint account to which he has contributed nothing for eight months. When he broke his leg, I made the horrible mistake of letting him move into the second bedroom. I wouldn't feel right about throwing him out in the street. An ideal solution would be to find him another home. Please print my name and telephone number. I need someone to take this charming moocher off my hands, and I'm not kidding.—*Miss——*, MUrryhill ——

Dear ——: Sorry, I can't print your name and telephone number. All some dames need to know is that a man is six feet tall, handsome, and a good dancer and they would grab him, secure in the knowledge that they could overlook his petty faults and turn him into an ideal husband.

The next letter is a good illustration of what I was talking about:

Dear Ann Landers: My husband died ten months ago and left me well off financially. I'm sixty-three but could pass for younger. I'm well traveled, well read, and there might be a little snow on the roof, but there's still a fire in the furnace. Please don't think me vulgar, but I want a husband, and I'm willing to pay for him. There must be some attractive men around in their forties who are tired of working and want to relax a little. Please don't tell me to wait for some nice gentleman to come along and marry me for myself. Why would a good-looking, middle-aged man want a sixty-three-year-old widow when he can have a twenty-eight-year-old divorcee? I know at least five wealthy widows who are pathetic in their loneliness. Why shouldn't I buy my way out of this circle if I can? Please give me some down-to-earth, practical advice. —*Lonely And Miserable*

Dear Gypsy: If you think you're "lonely and miserable" now, just marry some good-looking, middle-aged man who "wants to relax a little." No man worth his salt would be remotely interested in your propostion. Your "For Sale" sign would attract nothing but bums. The next letter is one you ought to clip out and paste in your hatband, lady.

Dear Ann Landers: Lately I notice a lot of widows have been writing in and asking where all the eligible men are hiding. I speak from experience when I say some of those "eligible men" should be *left* in hiding. My husband died in 1955, and I got to feeling sorry for myself. I must have been crazy, Ann. I owned my own home, drove a new car, had a very nice income and money in the bank. I took lovely trips and did as I pleased. Then Fancy Dan (five years my junior) came along. He sent me roses, telephoned me three times a day, and made me feel like sweet sixteen. I married him six months later, and here's the way it is now: He owes me $10,000 which he lost on a phony oil deal. The housekeeper I had for fifteen years quit because he criticized her ironing. A son he forgot to tell me about turned up and has been living in my home for three months, waiting to be drafted. I sit at the dinner table while the two of them talk past me like I was a wax dummy or something. If you print my letter, don't use the name of the city. Just sign me—*Had It Good And Didn't Know It.*

Dear Ann Landers: The high cost of living has put me behind the eight ball. No matter how I try, it is impossible to maintain a good address and decent clothes and have money left to drive a car and do some interesting things. I am twenty-nine years old, unmarried, very good looking, and an engaging conversationalist. I would like to make myself available (to high-type women only) for thirty dollars an evening plus expenses. I want only to serve as an escort, so please don't assume anything beyond that. I have a new Corvette and well-cut clothes. Hundreds of women sit at home simply because they do not know an attractive, respectable man who will take them out. I could give a woman a wonderful evening in exchange for this modest stipend. Will you help me to help them and myself at the same time?—*R.D.*

Dear R.D.: If a dame doesn't have thirty dollars,

how much would you charge for her to stand at the curb and watch you drive by?

Dear Ann Landers: I was very much interested in the letter from the man who described himself as twenty-nine, goodlooking, and an engaging conversationalist. He wanted to make himself available as an escort (to quality women only) for thirty dollars an evening plus expenses. No doubt you have received a tremendous response from women who are interested in acquiring his services. As a matter of fact, I'll bet the gentleman can't possibly accommodate them all. So, Ann, I would like to take the overflow, for twenty dollars an evening, plus expenses. I don't want to brag, but I have often been mistaken for Dean Martin. I, too, have a new car and well-cut clothes. The other fellow emphasized his intellectual qualities. I am more the physical type. I play a fine game of tennis and badminton, enjoy swimming and dancing. I would, of course, be willing to cut you in for putting my letter in the paper and fowarding the names of the lonesome ladies. Thank you.—*R.D. No. 2*

Dear R.D.: Don't stand on one foot waiting for the names of the lonesome ladies, Buddy Boy. This isn't that kind of a column.

Dear Ann Landers: Ours is an unusual problem. We will change the names, but I don't think we will fool anyone in our town. Our daughter is going with a nice young man. He works for a relative who is a funeral director. When Delbert comes to call on our daughter he sometimes drives over in the hearse. My husband and I do not like the looks of the hearse in front of our house. It creates a lot of talk among the neighbors, and sometimes strangers who are passing by just stand around and look. We mentioned this to Delbert, and he said, "A hearse is nothing to be ashamed of. It's a part of my job." My husband and I would be so much happier if Delbert would walk to our place or take a bus. What is your opinion?—*Mr. and Mrs.*

Dear M and M: Since the hearse is part of Delbert's job and he is not ashamed of it, tell him to park it in front of *his* house. You have the right to ask the young man to use more conventional transportation, and I hope you will.

Dear Ann Landers: I am a widow in my sixties and I am going with a widower the same age. Last Sunday, Zeke and I were out for a drive. He suggested going by his home and opening the windows to air the place out. I said, "Fine." After Zeke opened the windows he sat down on the couch, untied his shoelaces, and said, "It's so comfortable here I don't want to move. Why don't you walk home?" I thought he was joking because we were a good five miles from my house. I laughed and said, "Oh, stop it, Ezekiel." He replied, "I'm not kidding," and took off his shoes. I said goodbye and left. If you don't think five miles in Cuban heels is exhausting, try it. I arrived home thoroughly done in and half sick. Two hours later, Zeke showed up at my place—furious. He said he never dreamed I'd be that dumb. I asked why he didn't come after me. He said he thought I was sitting in his car. I'd like your opinion on who *is* the dumb one?—*Kalamazoo*

Dear Kalamazoo: Sounds like a tie to me.

Dear Ann Landers: In your column recently, a wife wrote that she was disturbed because her husband had come home from a stag party where two girls did strip acts. You told the wife she should not be thrown off balance by a "cheap little bimbo whose major talent is parading at stags in the altogether." For the first time in my life, I feel I should defend my profession. I have been an exotic dancer (I prefer this to "stripper") for twelve years. I am no cheap little bimbo but a hard-working woman who paid taxes on $40,000 last year. When I finished my schooling in the East at age sixteen, I went to work in the office of a major network. In the ten months I worked there, I received more indecent proposals and pinches on my posterior than in the twelve years I have been doing my act. There can be artistry and taste in exotic dancing. I am told I have a regal bearing which makes men respect me. The average male would think twice before he tried to pinch a woman who buys her own diamonds and minks, and travels with a 200-pound drummer. Since you claim to be fair, Ann, I hope you will print my letter and give the customers an eyeful.—*T.N.T.*

Dear Dynamite: I try always to be fair, and here is your letter. As for "giving the customers an eyeful," that's *your* line.

Dear Ann Landers: Nine of us girls belong to a poker club. We've been meeting every Tuesday night for almost fifteen years. The stakes are not high enough to hurt anyone, and we all have a good time. The newest member of the club is causing trouble. I will call her Zelda. We took her in last year when her husband died. Zelda has two artificial teeth in front. They are on a bridge. When Zelda is in a big pot she takes her teeth out and puts them on the chips for luck. You know as well as I do, Ann Landers, that the cards are going to fall where they are going to fall, but it is amazing the way Zelda's luck improves the minute she puts her teeth on the chips. The girls in the club don't like it—not because she wins, but because it is a disgusting sight. Please tell me what should be done.—*Yesterday's Hostess*

Dear Hostess: To dismantle onself in the presence of others is in the worst possible taste. Since Zelda seems to be compulsive about removing things, suggest that she put her earrings, beads, or wristwatch on the chips and leave her teeth in her head.

Dear Ann Landers: I'm writing about the girl who described her boyfriend as a "first-class gentleman" because he offered to pay for her abortion (which she later discovered she didn't need). This letter will probably sound like a Grade B movie or a rotten made-up story, but unfortunately it's true—every word. My mother died when I was sixteen, and I started sleeping with an older fellow. I told myself I was doing it because I missed my mother. I know now I did it because I was too dumb and too weak to say No. When I became pregnant, my boyfriend took me to an abortionist who botched the job and I almost died. Now I will never be able to have children. My "great lover" dropped me, and I took up with another bum who dragged me down into the gutter where I stayed for three miserable years. One day I woke up sick to death of myself and decided to get a respectable job. I am now twenty-nine years old, and I look forty-five. I avoid my school friends because I have made such a mess of my life I don't know what to say when we meet. I am tortured by the past and terrified of the future. I wrecked my life because of a foolish mistake. If just one girl learns something from this letter, perhaps my messed-up life will have served some purpose. Please print it.—*My Name Is Mud*

Dear Friend: You did not ask for advice, but I feel obliged to give it. Your inability to forgive yourself has set you on a course of self-destruction. Brooding and agonizing over past mistakes takes energy—energy that could be used to build a decent future. Professional help might be the answer if you are unable to do it alone. Get going.

Dear Ann Landers: The wife whose husband never takes his T-shirt off thinks *she* has a problem. Well, I'd give anything if I could trade troubles with her. My husband should keep his T-shirt on for the rest of his life. His tattoo decorations have been driving me out of my mind ever since we were married. His chest and arms read like the wall in a bus station men's room. When our children were young, it was impossible to divert their attention from "Daddy's pictures." They used to ask millions of questions, and my husband would just sit there like a wart on a pickle. I was the one who had to explain things. I can't count the number of times when we've been out with nice people, and after three drinks my husband peels off his shirt and shows off his art gallery. The next day he can't remember a thing. Believe me, Ann, it's not easy to keep decent friends when you have a husband who acts like that. I am not writing for advice because there is no solution to my problem. I am just writing to let you know that there are some very crazy people in this world, in case you don't already know it.—*Married To A Nut*

Dear Married: Thanks for writing. I already know it.

Seven

MEANWHILE, DOWN AT THE OFFICE

More people write to me from offices than from any other place of employment. One might consider this logical since office workers have easy access to a desk, stationery, a typewriter, stamps, and a handy mail chute. The factory worker, the hairdresser, the sales clerk, would not find it so convenient to write to Ann Landers—especially on company time.

There are other reasons for the disproportionate number of letters from office workers. An office is an ideal hatchery for love, sex, budding friendships, cutthroat competition, oneupsmanship, and making points with the boss. Moreover, the proximity of desks and the opportunity to communicate freely lends itself to intimacy.

Two daily coffee breaks provide gossip time. And what do people who work together gossip about? Each other, naturally.

The office party (which, I am pleased to report, is a vanishing tradition) has produced more letters to Ann Landers than any single holiday topic. This social atrocity is responsible for terminating an astonishing number of friendships. It has also created serious marital problems and does irreparable damage to the prestige of top executives, who, after several martinis, make jackasses of themselves and lose the respect of their employees.

And meanwhile, down at the office. . .

Dear Ann Landers: A girl I will call Rozetta has been my husband's secretary for three years. Rozetta is not just a secretary; she is more like an office manager. My husband says she has helped make his branch the best in the country and he owes her a great deal. Almost every Sunday my husband drives Rozetta to her sister's place, about forty miles from here. She stays there overnight and takes the bus back Monday morning. My husband is gone about three hours in all. I think this is out of line and have told him I would gladly pay the lady's bus fare out of my allowance if he would stop driving her. He insists the personal touch of going out of his way to do something nice for Rozetta is what makes it so meaningful. What do you say?—*Minnie*

Dear Minnie: I say the personal touch is a touch too personal. If your husband wants to do something nice for his secretary, tell him to try money.

Dear Ann Landers: My wife works in an office, and I am employed in a plant. We used to take the same bus to and from town, and it worked out fine. A few months ago, Wilma's boss decided to stagger the quitting time so there wouldn't be a crush at five, and now she takes an earlier bus. She is always home when I get there. Last night, I left work twenty minutes early because I had a backache. When the bus stopped at Wilma's corner, she boarded with a good-looking, well-built guy. They seemed to be having a great time, laughing and joking. When Wilma saw me, she got red in the face and introduced me. I recognized the plaid shirt he was wearing because I had ironed it. Wilma has been bringing home this guy's shirts for months—said they belonged to some orphan kid she wanted to help out. Wilma does all the washing in the family, and I do the ironing because I was a presser in the Navy. When we got home, I got mad and told her I wasn't ironing any more of the "orphan's" shirts. She called me a jealous fool and acted highly insulted. What do you make of this?—*Manny*

Dear Manny: This is indeed a new wrinkle—one that Wilma ought to iron out. She sounds like a big-hearted girl, but I think in the interest of peace and tranquility the "orphan" should carry his laundry to a commercial place.

Dear Ann Landers: I have rewritten this letter four times in an effort to make it printable. Please publish it, because I cannot receive a reply in the mail. There are these two women in our office. One is a divorcee, the other has never been married. They do not live together, but they have lunch together every day, take vacations together, and spend their evenings together. There are stories going around that these women have an abnormal relationship. I find it difficult to believe because they are both extremely intelligent and refined. Also the divorcee has two children. Could the rumors be true? If they are, should the women be fired?—*Upholder Of Decency*

Dear Up: You are asking if it is possible that the women are lesbians. The answer is, Yes—it is possible, but not necessarily true. Should they be fired? No. Not if they are competent—it would be cruel to deprive them of employment.

Dear Ann Landers: Please say something about people who chew gum with their mouths wide open. A woman in our office—we call her the Old Corn Popper—has this obnoxious habit, and she is driving us all nuts. Not only does the gum go crackle, snap, pop, but the dentures go clickety-click-clack until you could go out of your gourd. Can it be that she doesn't hear her-self? Please print this letter, Ann. I will tack it up on our bulletin board.—*SOS*

To Whom It May Concern: If you are reading this from an office bulletin board and have gum in your mouth, you may be "Old Corn Popper"—so watch it!

Dear Ann Landers: I've been working in this office for three years. Six girls have gotten married right under my nose, but nothing exciting ever happens to me. About three months ago a very nice young man was transferred here as supervisor for our section. He is clean-cut, pleasant, mannerly, and just my type. During working hours he pays a lot of attention to me, but when five o'clock comes he seems to vanish into thin air. For the last three week he has been coming by my desk after lunch. He always brings me a sack of peanuts. Do you think this means anything? Please ad-vise.—*Torchy*

Dear Torch: I once knew a man who bought a sack of peanuts every day for the monkeys in the zoo, but so far as I know he never asked any of them out.

Dear Ann Landers: Our office is what you might call a real swingin' little group. It turns out that four girls, including myself, have been played like crazy, one against the other, by a junior executive. He is tall, dark, and handsome, and has the morals of an alley cat and is also loose of lip. When I came to work here several months ago, I fell like a ton of teakwood. Nothing I saw or heard discouraged me. I knew he was dating three other girls in the office, and I knew, too, he was blabbing about how he had scored. I thought surely he'd be discreet about *me* because I'm the only girl who is not married, but I was mistaken. Four of us gals had dinner together, and we had an old-fashioned, shoes-off, hair-down "tell all." The dirty dog, it turns out, has been using the same line on all of us, right down to the romantic phrases and pet names. I'd like to fix his clock. Any ideas?—*Fuming*

Dear Fuming: His clock seems to be working just dandy. You're the one who is getting the works, dummy.

Dear Ann Landers: My boss is separated but not divorced. He is intrigued with my knowledge of American literature and wants to get to know me better. We can't talk in the office. He says it would be damaging to my reputation if I were seen in public with him, since he is still legally married. Last week he suggested that we go to a motel and just talk. I agreed. We have gone to this motel twice. Nothing out-of-the-way has happened. I think it is wonderful that he is so considerate of my reputation, but I feel uncomfortable checking into a motel with a man. I am reluctant to tell him "no more motel" because he may stop seeing me and I've grown fond of him. Any advice?—*Lady Guinevere*

Dear Lady Guinevere: I've often wondered what happened to Sir Galahad. Now I know. You've got him! How lucky can one girl get? It's not every boss who will invest in a motel room to protect a girl's reputation. Naturally everyone is blind and no one sees you go into the motel or leave. His car, of course, is invisible, so no one sees that either. Tell Sir Galahad you are concerned about *his* reputation, and knock it off.

Dear Ann Landers: About three months ago I hired the daughter of a friend to do secretarial work. She's a poor typist, handles the phone poorly, can't spell, and she has never heard of the comma. "Lady Astor" came in late three mornings last week and takes three hours for lunch. Her father has done me many favors and I value his friendship. He would be very unhappy if I fired her. He believes she is brilliant and has told me repeatedly that she loves her job. Please answer in the paper. The moron opens my mail.—*In A Spot*

Dear Spot: You have on your payroll a girl who can't spell, type, or handle the phone, comes in late and takes three hours for lunch. And you call *her* a moron? Give "Lady Astor" her walking papers. A friendship that hinges on keeping an incompetent relative isn't worth worrying about.

Dear Ann Landers: I'm a middle-aged career girl who enjoys her work and her life. A friend just phoned for the second time this week; she has a fellow she wants me to meet. Why don't people leave me alone? Why don't these do-gooders understand that many unmarried women are single by choice? I have a fascinating job, a beautiful apartment, good clothes, one great vacation a year, and I wouldn't trade places with any married woman. I see them at the office, rushing around like crazy trying to perform their wifely chores during lunch hour. They dash out of the door at 4:59 to do the marketing, fix supper, iron shirts and scrub floors. The married girls in this office look beat and run-down at the heels. They are helping to pay for *his* boat, or a car, or fishing and hunting gear, not to mention liquor and other odds and ends. And then, of course, there are the in-laws. I could go on and on but by now you have the idea. I wish others would get it, too. Thanks for letting me unload.—*Unclaimed Jewel By Choice*

Dear Unclaimed: The married girls are also married by choice. Not everyone wants a life in double harness. But if you haven't tried it, don't knock it.

Dear Ann Landers: I am twenty-eight, attractive, and the mother of three children. My husband and I have never had any serious trouble—until now. The top man in this organization has taken a liking to me. He is in his forties, good-looking, sophisticated, and married. This outfit has frequent social get-togethers. The boss always invites me to sit next to him and makes a fuss over me. Whenever there is music he dances my feet off. I try to be nice, if you know what I mean. Last night after an evening with the big shots, my husband blew his top. He told me he didn't need to have his wife play up to the boss to get ahead. My husband made some very strong statements, and I don't know how to handle the problem. Do you?—*Junior Executive's Wife*

Dear Wife: This story is as old as the gray flannel suit. Since you are now aware that your husband resents the boss's attentiveness, I suggest you cut down the voltage on your responses.

Dear Ann Landers: I'm a woman past fifty who has given the better part of her life to her job and her company. I was never married, and in a moment you will know why. I am the private secretary to the president of the firm. He is an attractive, well-to-do-bachelor sixty-eight years of age. I've been in love with him for twenty-two years, but he is unaware of my feelings. Our relationship has been a close one professionally, and he treats me with the greatest respect. I am well paid and I love my work, but it is becoming increasingly difficult to keep my love for this man disguised. I should have made my feelings known years ago, but there is no point in trying to relive the past. Would I be making a fool of myself if I told him now? Yes, I am prepared to leave if he thinks it best.—*Old Faithful*

Dear Old Faithful: If the man felt about you as you feel about him, he would have let you know it. Now

you at least have your self-respect. Don't unravel a tale
of twenty-two years of unrequited love at this late
date. It would sound bizarre and make the man uncomfortable in your presence.

Dear Ann Landers: When a wife says her husband
is home every night and he has given her no reason to
question his fidelity, then suddenly she finds a woman's
sweater and a pair of high-heeled shoes in the back
seat of the car, she *should* confront him with it. I was
in the same spot a few years ago and luckily an unexpected turn of events saved me. My husband went to
New Orleans to attend a convention. The boys thought
it would be cute to slip a pair of black lace panties into
his suitcase. Of course I found the panties when I un-
packed. They had been strategically placed with his
pajamas. When I handed the "evidence" to him, he
swore he knew nothing about it. I didn't believe him
and said so. Then the phone rang. One of his buddies
who was in on the prank had told his wife about it.
She persuaded him the gag might lead to trouble, so he
called me to apologize. If I had said nothing and that
phone call had not come, I would have believed the
worst.—*Bonnie*

Dear Ann Landers: I'm a blue-eyed brunette raised
on a farm near Alpena, Michigan. I came to Detroit,
got a job as secretary, and fell in love with a prominent executive in the auto industry. Greg was evasive
about where he lived, but I never pushed it. Yesterday
he telephoned to say he had the flu and couldn't keep
our date. I decided to surprise him with a honey and
lemon syrup my grandmother used to make. I got his
address from the office manager. Greg was sick all
right, and when he opened the door and saw me, he
got a whole lot sicker. The first thing I noticed was a
satin housecoat and some ostrich feather bedroom slip-

pers. He said, "I know what you're thinking and you're wrong. That stuff belongs to a sweet kid from Sheboygan who is out of work and needed a place to stay. She'll be out of here tomorrow." I called him a liar and left. When I got home the phone was ringing. He begged me to believe him. Would you?—*Egg On My Face*

Dear Egg: Would I believe your big hearted Romeo is playing housemother to a busted kid from Sheboygan? No, I would not. And neither should you.

Dear Ann Landers: I was shocked recently when at a social gathering an officer of a bank had one too many highballs and began to discuss the financial problems of two of his clients. Last night at another social affair a nurse who is employed in a doctor's office revealed some highly personal information about a prominent woman who is a patient. I always thought individuals who dealt with the public had a moral obligation to keep their mouths shut. It seems unspeakable that they would use confidential information for social chitchat. Is there something I, as one person, can do to combat this sort of thing? I am—*Horrified And Fuming*

Dear Horrified: Yes. You can do business with another bank and go to another doctor. And if the question is ever raised as to why, you can explain, leaving out names, of course.

Here's one about another "public servant" whose mouth goes on active duty when he meets up with the joy juice:

Dear Ann Landers: What do you think of a man who is a bookkeeper in a credit union and goes around telling everybody (after three martinis) how much everybody owes? I don't owe the credit union anything, but some of my friends do and I feel sorry for them. Should I tip off the chief executive who would have Mr. Blabbermouth fired at once? Frankly I dislike the man intensely, but I don't want to be responsible for causing him to lose his job.—*Bix*

Dear Bix: If Mr. Blabbermouth has been talking through his martinis for several months, his days are numbered. Keep quiet and let one of the injured parties give him the ax.

Dear Ann Landers: My husband is a bright, hardworking young man. He is also wildly ambitious, determined to wind up on top of the financial heap regardless of what it takes. Several months ago he went to work for a firm which offered him a fine salary and an opportunity to advance in his field. It has been two years since we made the move, and my husband is deeply disappointed in the firm and quite articulate about his disappointment. It embarrasses me when he speaks disparagingly about his bosses even though what he says is true. I've tried to tell him it's neither wise nor honorable, but I might as well talk to the wall. Can you help?—*A Young Wife*

Dear Wife: This is what Elbert Hubbard has to say on the subject. Clip it out for your husband. It may change his approach. "If you must growl, condemn, and eternally find fault, resign your position, and when you are on the outside, damn to your heart's content. But so long as you are a part of the institution do not condemn it, or the first high wind that comes along will blow you away and you will never know why."

Dear Ann Landers: Recently you had a letter in your column from a church secretary who complained because the minister wore his hat in the office. That letter gave me courage to write about a gripe which is extremely annoying. My boss is bright, attractive, well-educated, and going places. At the close of his conversations with other businessmen he invariably says, "Bye-bye." I don't know what *they* think of this, but to me it makes him sound like a case of arrested development. I have discussed this with other secretaries and they agree it's ridiculous. Should I come right out and tell my boss "bye-bye" is no way to end a business conversation?—*Ready To Flip*

Dear Ready: If your boss wants to express his own personality rather than stick to conventional phrases, why should you become unhinged? Say nothing. If you just can't bear it another minute, go to his office and tell him, "Bye-bye."

Dear Ann Landers: There's a woman who works in this office who thinks she is Queen Elizabeth. Her desk is on the aisle. Since she has been here since the Year One, the boss, out of respect for old age, introduces her to all the big shots who come this way. It is sickening the way she rises to her feet and extends her hand with a regal flourish. Isn't this bad manners? Shouldn't a woman remain seated and wait for the gentleman to extend *his* hand? How about putting the ignoramus straight?—*B.D. And C.*

Dear B.D.: Sorry, but the queen is right. It's perfectly proper for a woman to stand at her desk when being introduced to a person of importance. And, of course, the woman always extends her hand first.

Dear Ann Landers: My husband works in an office which employs twenty-five men and women. In the past two years three of his co-workers have had weddings in their families. In all instances a blanket invitation was posted on the office bulletin board. The employees all chipped in for gifts. My husband and I attended two of the three weddings. About six other employees attended also. Our son is being married in the spring. My husband thinks we should follow the office procedure and post an invitation on the bulletin board. I never felt this was proper, but he says we must not hurt anyone's feelings. He says, "When in Rome, do as the Romans do." We would appreciate it, Ann, if you would help us decide.—*Perplexed*

Dear Perplexed: The Romans did plenty that wasn't worth imitating, so forget about that phrase. A notice on the office bulletin board is OK for informing employees that the coffee machine is on the bum, but it's no way to invite people to a wedding. Send personal invitations in the mail, and confine the invitations to those you want to invite.

Dear Ann Landers: I am personnel director of a large company. We are proud of our plant, our superior equipment, and the benefits we provide for our employees. Yet every day at least one woman comes into my office and cries all over the upholstered furniture. A female who accepts the challenge of the business world should expect criticism, competition, and personality conflicts. She asked for the whole package when she left her comfortable home and went out after that paycheck. I'd like to buy a full-page ad in every newspaper in the country and say, "WOMEN WHO WORK—GROW UP. Men cannot respect a woman who blubbers like a four-year-old when things go wrong." I must sign off now. Here comes another one.—*Damp Furniture*

Dear Damp Furniture: All right, girls, turn off the waterworks, you're ruining the personnel director's shoeshine. And you, sir, keep those paper tissues handy because the gals are going to keep right on bawling.

Dear Ann Landers: I have worked in this office for fourteen years. At least twice a month someone comes around with a small speech: "Marty's mother died. Would you pitch in fifty cents for flowers?" Or, "Sara is getting married on Saturday. Would you care to give a dollar toward a wedding gift?" Or, "Hank is in the hospital. We are sending him a couple of books." I have never said No. Two weeks ago tragedy struck a member of my family. My co-workers did not send flowers, or even a card. Should I turn the other cheek? Or should I inform the secretary who is in charge of collections that I am fed up?—*Put Out*

Dear Put Out: You don't tell me whether the relative was a parent, a sister, a brother, a grandmother, or a cousin. The relationship could make a difference. Then, too, perhaps the secretary did not know of your loss. If I were you, I'd say nothing. Consider all the possibilities and continue to give, if and when you wish.

Dear Ann Landers: I had to smile when I read the letter from the secretary whose boss couldn't keep his hands to himself. She said his "fatherly" pats had become bold pinches and squeezes, and she wanted your advice on how to keep him in line without jeopardizing her job. It so happens that I am a boss, and my problem is a secretary who won't keep her hands off *me*. I am fifty-nine and no handsome lover-type. My secretary is twenty-nine and extremely attractive. She is also very competent and knows this office from top to bottom. If I fired her, it would take months to train a new girl. This pawing has been going on for nine years. Please tell me what to do. I am in urgent need of an answer.—*Also Upacrick*

Dear Also: If you have been "suffering" with the same problem for nine years, it can't be very urgent. I will give you the same advice I gave that secretary: Kwitcherkiddin'.

Eight

STICKS AND STONES

". . . can break my bones but words can never hurt me." This familiar childhood taunt is the feebler disclaimer of one whose feelings have been hurt. It has a nice ring to it but very little truth.

Words can do more than wound. They can destroy. Every sack of my mail contains letters from victims of words. Twisted words repeated with malice, savage words uttered in anger, foolish words born of ignorance. And there is considerable evidence to support Goethe's sardonic statement: "When ideas fail, words can be a convenient substitute."

A phrase can elevate the blood pressure, produce temporary deafness or start a five-alarm family fight. Some of the best-known catalysts are these:

"When I was your age—"

"I'm going to tell you something for your own good—"

"Give me the keys to the car. You are in no condition to drive—"

After examining battle patterns for a dozen years, it is obvious that a surprising number of people consciously or unconsciously use anger-provoking phrases because they prefer a violent argument to being ignored. "When he fights with me he is acknowledging my presence" is the way a Fort Wayne reader put it.

This chapter tells of trouble that started with a few ill-chosen words. The point here is best exemplified in

112

the old Russian adage: "You are the master of the unspoken word. Once the word has passed your lips, you are no longer the master—you are the slave."

Dear Ann Landers: The letter from the man complaining about his idiot wife who was a Radcliffe graduate sounds like my husband wrote it. Yes, I let the bath water run over occasionally while I get to talking on the phone. And I don't deny that I sometimes forget where I put the keys, the baseball gloves, and even the kids. But when a person is emotionally upset he can forget his own name. I'm lucky not to be completely cuckoo considering what I put up with from that jerk. To begin with, he is envious because I am a college graduate, and he flunked out of Swarthmore in his sophomore year. Whenever I attend an alumni meeting, he says I am reverting to my second childhood. I've stuck by him through one raunchy affair after another. He has run the female gamut, from sixteen to sixty. The man simply loathes work. If he weren't working for his father, he'd be on unemployment compensation. I'm forgetful. So what? What I'd *really* like to forget is that I was stupid enough to tie up with this baboon.—*Also Radcliffe*

Dear Also: Thanks for writing. You have my sympathy.

Dear Ann Landers: What does one say to children when they ask questions about an aunt who lives in a beautiful apartment, drives a new car every two years, wears elegant clothes, exquisite jewelry and furs, and doesn't have a job? The truth is she's the great and good friend of a rich old coot who is married. Rita has a nice personality and behaves like a lady. She is generous to her widowed mother and is always there with her checkbook when someone in the family needs help. I guess you'd call her a good egg. But this doesn't alter the fact that she is a kept woman. What do I tell my children?—*Stuck For An Explanation*

Dear Stuck: Tell your children Aunt Rita is good to her widowed mother, is always there with her checkbook when someone in the family needs help, and that she is a good egg.

Dear Ann Landers: When I was married in 1954, I weighed 98 pounds. Unfortunately, I gained 30 pounds with each of my two children, and the weight just stayed on. Today I weigh 158 but I really don't look it. When I put on my good corset and wear heels and a black dress, you'd guess me at about 130. My husband makes me miserable because I am overweight. Every time I reach for a second piece of butter or a baked potato, he makes an ugly remark. He is one of those wiry types who can still get into his Korean War uniform. Last Sunday he put it on to do the yard work just to make me mad. Why should I deprive myself of food to please a man who is so mean? I know several women who are overweight, but their husbands love them anyway. Please say he should accept me as I am. I get very depressed over his constant nagging.—*Pleasingly Plump*

Dear Plump: Some husbands don't care if their wives get fat, but your husband *does* care and he has let you know it. Obviously, you'd rather stuff your face than please him. This hurts a man's pride, and the needling is his way of getting even. One of these days I hope you get sick of yourself and go to a doctor and ask to be put on a sensible diet. When you begin to shed those unhealthy, unattractive pounds, your husband will like you better, and you'll like yourself better, too.

Ann Landers: We are not calling you "Dear" Ann Landers because we don't think you are dear. We think you are just rotten. This letter is being written by three twelve-year-old women who will never read your crummy column again as long as we live. Your advice to the mother who wrote and asked if her thirteen-year-old daughter should be allowed to go to a dance with a sixteen-year-old boy has made you a lot of enemies. Don't you know that some thirteen-year-old girls are very mature and have a lot of sense? Age isn't everything. I know better than *that,* and I won't be thirteen until July. We think you should get your brains out of mothballs and catch up with 1968 activities or turn your job over to a person who is living in this century. And just in case you think we are cheap, hoody girls, we would like you to know that we are all refined young ladies who come from very rich families. *Ex-Readers*

Dear Refined Ladies From Rich Families: Since you are no longer reading the column I don't expect you to see this, but perhaps someone will tell you about it. I want to congratulate you on the ladylike manner in which you expressed yourselves. I could tell right away that you girls were the last word in refinement. The advice stands.

Dear Ann Landers: Marvin and I have been going together for over a year. We are both in our thirties and old enough to know what we are doing. Marvin was married briefly five years ago, but it didn't work out. Two weeks ago Marvin began to talk marriage. He made it clear that he was not actually proposing, just "considering it" because there were a few things he had to find out first. Tonight he asked me five questions which he had written down on a piece of paper. Here are the questions:

(1) Do you need any dental work done?

(2) Do you need any surgery?

(3) What kind of insurance do you carry?

(4) Are you in line to inherit any money?

(5) Is there any insanity in your family?

I like Marvin very much and we get along fairly well, but these questions have raised some doubt in my mind. What do you think?—*Miss D.*

Dear Miss: I think you don't need a nut like this for a husband. One thing is certain, it isn't necessary to ask *him* question No. 5. You already know the answer.

Dear Ann Landers: I have two children and I'm expecting my third in a few weeks. The problem is my sister Vera. Vera has been married eighteen years, but she has no children. Three years ago, Vera and her husband moved out of the state. She has come home quite often to help out when any of us had new babies and when Mamma was sick. Lately she's been writing such remarks as "Little ones wear me out. They make me nervous. I don't think I could take it the way I feel now." (Vera has a slight case of arthritis, but she is not crippled or anything like that.) I have the feeling she doesn't want to take care of my family when I go to the hospital and she's preparing me for the letdown. Ann, I feel it is my sister's Christian duty to help me out. Please tell her so.—*Troubled*

Dear Troubled: Christian duty, my eye. Just because a woman is childless doesn't mean she's obliged to be a nurse or a maid for her sister. Imposing on relatives causes more trouble in this world than any five problems combined. If your sister had offered to help you out, fine. Since she did not, make other arrangements.

Dear Ann Landers: I agree with your stand on wedding rings. They don't mean a thing. My husband's wedding ring left a very deep impression on me—or I should say on my lip—when he hit me during our honeymoon. Bruce was one of those beautifully mannered foreign phonies. He was the first one on his feet when a lady entered the room, the first one with the cigarette lighter, and the first one in the lifeboat. (We were on the *Andrea Doria*.) After a four-week courtship I married this royal four-flusher, and the wedding ring was *his* idea. I confess the double-ring ceremony sounded very romantic, and it was easy for me to agree to it. I am no longer married to Bruce, and you can bet your boots my present husband does *not* wear a wedding ring and he never will.—*Happy Now*

Dear Now: You realize, of course, the jewelers are going to hate us both, but I'm pleased that you support my position.

Dear Ann Landers: I need some help and I need it fast. Whenever I say to my thirteen-year-old, "That's enough TV, go do your homework," my husband yells, "Stop nagging the boy." When I tell my ten-year-old to go back upstairs and wash his neck, his dad shouts, "Don't be such a perfectionist. He's clean enough." Yesterday, my eleven-year-old came to the breakfast table in soiled trousers and a wrinkled shirt which he had worn for two days. I told him to change his clothes. His dad chimed in, "The boy looks all right. Stop picking on him." The kids get the idea I'm a witch left over from Halloween and their dad is a saint. What can I do?—*Defenseless*

Dear D.: The kids are smarter than you think. And they'll get smarter as time goes on. Children want discipline. It gives them a feeling of security. Your husband is deceiving himself if he thinks they'll love him for his leniency. He may appear to be winning the popularity contest on the home front, but in the long run he will lose out completely.

Dear Ann Landers: Last Sunday our family drove over one hundred miles to visit my brother, his wife, and their newborn son. Midway through dinner, my sister-in-law left the table to take care of her infant. When we finished the meal, she called for us to come and say good-bye. I almost fainted when I saw she was breast-feeding her baby. Since then, our children, who are eleven, nine, seven, and five years of age, have been bothering me with questions about sex. I am furious with my sister-in-law for placing me in this embarrassing position. I hadn't figured on mentioning sex to my children until they were older. This stupid woman *knew* we were leaving for home right after dinner. Why couldn't she have waited another thirty minutes to nurse her baby? I'd like to take this matter up with her, but I don't know what to say. Will you please lambaste her for rudely leaving the table and behaving in this repulsive manner in front of my children?—*Disgusted*

Dear Disgusted: If your children don't know how life begins and how infants are nourished by their mothers, it's time they learned. You say you planned on telling them when they were "older." How much older? Ask your doctor for some literature to guide you. And get going, or you'll have four kids who are as mixed up as you are, lady.

Dear Ann Landers: I was upset by the letter from the woman who wanted to tie her husband's jaws together with a silk stocking to keep him from snoring. Some women may think I'm nutty as a fruitcake, but the sound of my husband snoring is the sweetest sound I know. It tells me that he is at my side, where he belongs. Not only do I enjoy hearing him snore, but I love to look at his face when he is asleep. He looks so much like our son when he was a baby. There is a quality of innocence in his face that reduces me to mush. His hair is mussed up, like a little boy's, and his lips have a mischievous curve. My husband has no idea I like to watch him sleep, so please don't print my initials or the name of this city. Just sign me—*Mrs. Contented.*

Dear Mrs.: You sound like a lady in love. How lovely—for you both.

Dear Ann Landers: My wife announced unashamedly that she could not remain true to me because I am "low-key, undemonstrative, unaffectionate, and indifferent." Will you please tell me how a man can work up any enthusiasm for a hypocritical, sanctimonious, self-centered, detached, insensitive, erratic, twisted, stupid, unresponsive, uncommunicative, warped, sullen, capricious, unpredictable, deceitful, punitive, self-righteous, obstinate woman who has never been wrong about anything in her whole life? And don't tell me I need a doctor. What I need is a woman. —*Smart But Dumb*

Dear Smart But: You must be dumber than you are smart, or you would not have married a hypocritical, sanctimonious, self-centered, detached, insensitive, erratic, twisted, stupid, unresponsive, uncommunicative, warped, sullen, capricious, unpredictable, deceitful, punitive, self-righteous, obstinate woman who has never been wrong about anything in her whole life.

Dear Ann Landers: You printed a letter from a woman who complained because a friend monopolized every conversation with "I, me, mine, I did, I went, I bought, etc." Everyone knows someone who is similarly afflicted. Here is a simple essay that might help people get along together just a little better: The seven most important words in the English language are "I made a mistake and I'm sorry." The six most important words are "You did a very good job." The five most important words are "And what is your opinion?" The four most important words are "How can I help?" The three most important words are "I appreciate you." The two most important words are "Thank you." The least important word is "I.'—*J.D.K.*

Dear J.D.K.: I hope the wife of the man who wrote the next letter sees yours.

Dear Ann Landers: Whenever I apologize my wife says, "You aren't *really* sorry. You are just saying you are sorry to get me off your back." I've even gotten down on my knees and she still says, "I can tell by your face you don't mean it." Last week she bolted the front door from the inside and I couldn't get in, so I went to a hotel. I told her I almost broke my hand pounding, but she insists I didn't knock at all and I was looking for an excuse to stay out all night. When I said, "I'm sorry," she said, "You are not. You are glad." Why are some women like this?—*On The Defensive*

Dear Defensive: Because they can't bear to let a guy off the hook with a few sentences. They must keep the heat on indefinitely. Find a recording of that old song, "What Can I Say, Dear, After I Say I'm Sorry?" and play it at the appropriate time. It might appeal to her sense of humor—if she has one.

Dear Ann Landers: What makes an adult incapable of telling anything straight? I hate to call my husband a liar, but I am shocked by the way he deviates from the facts. Ned comes from a large family and they all have this despicable habit. I would never embarrass Ned in the presence of others and say, "No, dear, it wasn't like that," but I have pleaded with him in private to please stop exaggerating. It hasn't helped. Why?—*Pro-Truth*

Dear Pro: People who embroider the facts beyond recognition want to impress and/or amuse, and they don't trust the straight story to do the job. Exaggerators and distorters earn a reputation for irresponsibility or clownishness, and no one takes them seriously. This is a high price to pay for a brief moment in the spotlight.

Dear Ann Landers: Will you please tell me why a compliment sticks in some people's throat? I know Ben likes chopped herring the way his mother used to fix it. Believe me, it's a lot of trouble to bone and chop a herring, but I do it because I want to please him. Why can't he show a little appreciation when I go out of my way to do something nice? What would it cost him? Last night I said, "Ben, is the chopped herring good?" He answered, "I'm eating it, ain't I?" I said, "Yes, Ben, I can see you're eating it, but is it good?" He answered, "If it isn't good, then I'll tell you." Ben is a wonderful husband, but this one fault of his has been eating on me for thirty years. What should I do?—*Lucky I Don't Have Ulcers*

Dear Lucky: If the worst thing you can say about Ben is that he doesn't rave over your chopped herring, you are lucky. Pray for another thirty years together.

Dear Ann Landers: My husband is the type who must have the last word no matter what it costs him. Well, it is now costing him fifteen days in jail. It all started with a speeding ticket. My husband said he was not speeding, that the cop was laying for him. He refused to pay the ticket and went to court to plead not guilty. When the judge reminded my husband that he had been nabbed for speeding twice in the past two years, he got mad and called the judge a name. The judge gave him fifteen days. So now what am I to tell our six-year-old son? How will he feel if he knows his father is in jail? Will it scar him for life? I need answers and I need them now.—*Undone*

Dear Un: Tell your son that people who drive cars must follow the rules or pay the penalty, which in this case was a jail sentence. Make it clear that Daddy did not rob a bank or kill anyone but that he did break a law, and laws must be obeyed if we are to have a world safe for everybody.

Dear Ann Landers: What does an intelligent, successful man think he is proving when he swears every time he opens his mouth? My husband can't complete a sentence without putting a curse word in somewhere. Our daughters have asked him to please watch his language when guests are in the house, but it doesn't do any good. I've never heard the neighbors' husbands swearing up a storm out in the yard, but they've heard mine at least a dozen times this summer. Why does he do it, and what can I do to get him to stop?—*Mrs. M.*

Dear Mrs.: People who lace their language with profanity—and worse—are afraid their ideas are not strong enough. The habitual swearers actually become deaf to their own profanity. Nagging is ineffective. It's his problem. Don't let it become yours.

Dear Ann Landers: I'm a bachelor, forty-two, and have been keeping company for three years with a pleasant but not beautiful widow who is thirty-six. We live in the same apartment building. About five nights a week she'd have me in for dinner. (I must say she was a fine cook.) Three times in the last month when the telephone rang she'd pick it up and say, "I'm sorry but you have the wrong number." Once I stood near the phone and I heard a man's voice. After these calls she always seemed flustered. I began to suspect she was having an affair on the sly. I told her so in plain language. She broke down and cried and ordered me to leave—for good. I phoned her twice last week, but she was very distant and unfriendly. I guess I was a little hasty. Please help me fix things up.—*Red*

Dear Red: Finding restaurant food a bit expensive? How could this woman be having an affair behind your back when she was feeding your face in her apartment five nights a week? And when would she have time for "wrong numbers"? You were "hasty"? Well, she was slow. She should have given you the air long ago.

Dear Ann Landers: After twenty-five years of marriage I had to admit my wife was a bore. I met a younger woman who was exciting, attractive, and made me feel alive. When I asked my wife for a divorce, she took it like a lady and we parted friends. I am very happy. I pay alimony and child support, and I am never late with the check. The problem is my teenage children. They treat me as if I were a stranger. Is this fair? Everyone in town is aware of their indifference to me, and it is humiliating. After all, the problem was not with them. It was with my ex-wife. I would like your help.—*Texas Dad*

Dear Dad: I guess everything comes bigger in Texas —even the heels. Your children resent what you did to their mother, and they are letting you know it. Go cry on somebody else's shoulder, Tex.

Dear Ann Landers: Betsy and her whole family are peculiar people. Since she married my brother we are thrown together often because they are great believers in families being close. Betsy and her family speak Spanish. Whenever we are together my folks and I sit there like outsiders because we don't understand what is being said. We were raised where folks are hospitable and friendly. Is there any way we can let them know we feel uncomfortable when they speak a foreign language right in front of us? Maybe if they knew, they'd cut it out.—*Polly*

Dear Polly: Instead of sitting there, smoldering, why not let them know you want to learn a few words of their language? Try to teach them some English. It will break the sound barrier and you'll all wind up liking each other better. Communication is more than words. It's a smile, a look in the eye, and a warm feeling that never gets lost in the translation.

Dear Ann Landers: Your advice is usually excellent, but I think you could have done much better with your answer to the sixteen-year-old girl whose father said, "If you marry Clark you'll regret it because your children will be ugly, and it's not fair to give kids a handicap like that."

Haven't you noticed that some of the most beautiful people have ugly parents and some of the most gorgeous couples produce physically unattractive children?

What a child is going to look like is the biggest gamble known to mankind. It all depends on how the chromosomes and genes combine. If the little rascals that carry the worst features of both parents get together, you'll have a real loser. On the other hand, if the best features of two average-looking people collide you may get a raving beauty or a handsome boy.

So, why didn't you tell the girl to give her Dad *that* word, Ann?—*Got The Best From Both*

Dear Best: Because I didn't think of it, Buster. But I'm glad you did.

Dear Ann Landers: My father-in-law has been a widower since 1955. We hoped he would marry one of the fine women he has been taking out because soon he will be sixty years of age.

Last night he brought over a knock-kneed blonde who wore white lipstick, no eyebrows, and a red dress cut down to her navel. His first words were, "Meet the wife." My husband almost passed out. Finally he said, "Are you Dizzy Doris?" She giggled and answered, "Yes, but you can call me Mother."

Ann, my husband used to go to school with that girl. She is two years younger than he is. He couldn't stand her then, and he doesn't want her in our house now. I'm trying to keep peace in the family. Please help me.—*Befuddled*

Dear B: Since Doris is obviously your father-in-law's choice, Dizzy though she may be, you should both accept her.

Maintain the relationship on an invitation-only basis. Follow the directions on the jar of salad dressing: "Keep cool, but don't freeze."

Dear Ann Landers: I'm a married woman, forty-four, with a lovely family. I've known for six months that I need surgery. I have been putting it off until I've run out of excuses. The reason I am avoiding the operation is that I'm afraid of what I might say under an anesthetic. My husband is the attentive type who would insist on being with me every minute. If I started to talk, I could ruin myself. I can't discuss this with anyone for obvious reasons. Please tell me what to do. There must be a solution, but I don't see it—*D. Prest*

Dear D.: You can discuss this with your doctor in complete confidence. The problem will not be new to him. (It isn't new to me, either.) You have several alternatives. The simplest solution would be for your doctor to bar all relatives from the hospital until your surgery has been completed and you have regained consciousness.

Dear Ann Landers: Our six-year-old came home from school yesterday in tears. He tried to avoid me by going straight to his room. It took awhile but finally I persuaded him to tell me what was bothering him. The child had accidentally wet his pants during class. The teacher ridiculed him before all the boys and girls. She called him a baby and said he should be ashamed of himself. He was not permitted to join in the play period but was made to stand alone, his face to the wall. Now the boy doesn't want to go back. He's a high-strung youngster to begin with, and I fear this incident will have a damaging effect on his attitude toward school. What should be done?—*Heartsick In Alabama*

Dearheart: If all youngsters in Alabama who wet their pants in school during a single day were lined up, it would be a long damp line, indeed. I hope you will go to school and speak to the principal about the teacher who humiliated the boy. She needs educating.

Dear Ann Landers: We christened our son "Blair" because it is a distinguished family name. We wanted him to carry it with pride. Somewhere along the line, he picked up the nickname "Runt." Now, at age fourteen, this is what everyone calls him. At this very moment, he has five friends in the game room. I do not know the given name of any of these boys. All I hear is "Bud," "Crunch," "Red," "Bowser," and "Skinny." A name can be very important in creating an image. How can a young man have a promising legal career when he is burdened with an undignified handle like "Runt"? Do you agree?—*Connecticut Yankee*

Dear Yankee: A boy nicknamed "Whizzer" did all right. Don't worry, Mother. If Runt has what it takes, the world will be happy to take what he has.

The next writer also has a name problem, different in nature, but a problem nonetheless:

Dear Ann Landers: Am I crazy? I am going with a wonderful fellow who has an odd last name. Most people, when they see the name in print, pronounce it incorrectly, and it comes out like a dirty four-letter word. Would I be way out of line to ask my boyfriend to change the spelling of his name so people would not become so embarrassed? I've seen folks stammer and get red in the face, afraid to even try it.—*A Blusher*

Dear Blusher: Has the boy asked you to marry him? Have you said Yes? If so, I see nothing wrong in asking him to change the spelling of his name because it will be your name, too. If you don't plan to marry him, honey, keep quiet. The problem is a temporary one.

Dear Ann Landers: My wife is a great gal and we get along just fine. The only real problem is that Jessie is insanely jealous. I couldn't cheat on Jessie even if I wanted to (which I don't) because she knows where I am every minute, and I am never any place I shouldn't be. The other day I made some harmless remark about a waitress like, "That's what I call a built broad." Jessie blew her stack right there in the restaurant. Last night it happened again. We were at a party and one of the guests brought her sister from Toledo. All I said was, "That girl should never wear anything but a sweater for two very good reasons." Jessie yanked me into the other room and told me if I didn't stop talking rotten, she would "take steps." Honest, Ann, I am just a fun-loving guy who doesn't mean any harm. If you have any suggestions on how I can get along better with my wife, I'd like to hear them.—*Eight Ball*

Dear Eight: There's an old Hebrew expression that might not come off in English, but I think you'll get the idea: "If you don't want to hear a cat yowl, don't step on its tail." It sounds as if you two and the couple in the next letter should stay out of restaurants.

Dear Ann Landers: Last night we were in a small café, and a loud drunk in the next booth kept hogging the jukebox and playing the same record over and over. When I asked him to knock it off, he said he liked the record and planned to play it at least a dozen times more. I told him my girl hates the record and it was giving her a headache. He called her a mopey, bowlegged broad, so I let him have it right in the kisser. The owner of the restaurant threw us out. Now my girl says she wants nothing to do with a roughneck who fights in public.—*Frank*

Dear Frank: Consider yourself lucky you didn't get your profile changed. Some guys act drunk but they fight sober. You should have left the place if you didn't like the music. Promise to use your head instead of your dukes in the future, and I will ask your girl to give you another chance. OK? OK.

Dear Ann: I just read the letter signed Frank, and your advice was lousy. It is a gentleman's place to protect his wife or his girl. When that drunk called Frank's girl friend a mopey, bowlegged broad, he had every right to belt him in the kisser. Your suggestion that Frank was a roughneck and that he and his girl should have left the restaurant was strictly for the birds. Why don't you ask your husband what *he* would have done if somebody called you a mopey, bowlegged broad?— *More Than Frank*

Dear More: I asked my husband, and he said he hasn't hit a guy since he was in the sixth grade, and he is in no shape to start taking on drunks in restaurants. Any more questions?

Nine

DOLLAR$ AND ENE

Money is not necessarily the root of all evil. In fact, people who have been both rich and poor insist that rich is better.

One might assume that a column such as mine would attract heavy mail from readers in financial trouble, but such is not the case. Although I receive a great many letters about money, surprisingly few people complain about not having enough.

At least half the money problems I hear about come from readers who have lent money to a friend or a relative and can't seem to get it back.

The pattern is fascinating because it defies all laws of logic. Here is a typical situation: An individual (or a couple) is faced with an emergency. A mortgage comes due—illness in the family—someone needs plane fare to go to his mother's funeral. The man in the spot asks a buddy to come to the rescue. The favor is granted and the money is handed over—on good faith alone—nothing in writing. The grateful friend has promised to repay the money "as soon as possible." There are handshakes all around, and sometimes tears of gratitude. The atmosphere is one of congeniality and fine fellowship. The grateful friend is relieved and jubilant. The benevolent buddy is delighted he could "help out."

Weeks pass. Then months. No effort is made to

repay the loan. Benevolent Buddy notices that Grateful Friend seems to be avoiding him. After a few gentle and unsuccessful attempts to collect, it becomes obvious that the relationship isn't what it used to be. After several months, Grateful Friend and Benevolent Buddy are barely speaking. When the victim writes to Ann Landers, he puts it this way: "My reward for being bighearted and trusting the guy is a broken friendship and a hole in my bank account." He signs his letter, "Took Schnook."

Do I subscribe to Shakespeare's advice, "Neither a borrower nor a lender be—"? No. I do not regard this as a viable philosophy. Not all people are deadbeats. To assume such a cynical attitude is to take a markdown on the whole human race. But, more important, a life that precludes helping others is sterile, selfish, and meaningless. The solution, then, is to lend a helping hand, but on a businesslike basis. Something in writing can be very useful when memories fail and the warmth of gratitude begins to cool.

The notion that most wives are irresponsible and slightly addlebrained when it comes to handling money is a myth. My mail indicates that in a great many instances the budget is shot because the husband is the fiscal idiot.

Occasionally, I will receive a letter from a husband who writes, "My wife is trying to put us in the poorhouse. She buys everything she sees." But the letters from frantic wives whose husbands are wildly extravagant outnumber the boys' 50 to 1. For example, "Joe went out and bought another motorcycle. We still owe on the doctor bill from his last bike accident. Last year he spent $350 on fishing equipment and $700 on a boat."

Writing this column has taught me something about

the role money plays in the lives of men and women. While a scarcity of money can be a serious hardship, it does not cause misery and heartache so long as there are compensating balances. Millions of men and women struggle along, making do, doing without, stretching the paycheck, and scratching as best they can to make ends meet.

They sometimes complain, but they do not break down. Some human element, a good wife or husband, children who need and love them, keeps these people from cracking up.

On the other hand I hear from hundreds of women who have beautiful homes, elegant wardrobes, and unlimited financial resources, but they are depressed and rudderless. They can find no reason to go on living. Money has provided them with comfort and luxury, and life is easy. And perhaps this is where the trouble lies. For many, life is *too* easy. People need to be needed. When there is nothing to strive for, no goals, no challenges, the zest for living is gone.

Dear Ann Landers: Here I am, ready to lie down on your couch, and nobody is more surprised than I. I went with this heel for three years, and when I say "went with," I mean I devoted myself to him, body and soul. I invested part of my inheritance in his business, which failed. When he was down on his luck, I let him move into my apartment and I moved in with my aunt. Last January he went into a nutty business that clicked. Instead of giving back my $5,000, he bought himself a new car. Yesterday he gave me the big news. He has decided he's not good enough for me and I should find someone who is. His last words were,

"Baby, you deserve the best and I hope you get it." I hear he is seeing a wealthy widow who is old enough to be his mother. Should I invest in a private eye and throw the book at him?—*Crushed*

Dear Crushed: What book? Dun & Bradstreet? It's the only book that would interest the jerk. If he marries that rich widow for her money, he'll earn every dime of it. It's the hardest work there is.

Dear Ann Landers: I was deeply disappointed in your answer to "Oys-Gashpilt." The poor gal was sick and tired of carrying the financial load for her husband. You gave her precious little comfort. To begin with, I don't know if you speak German but "Oys-Gashpilt" means "played-out." After twenty-five years of pullin' that barge and totin' that bale, it's easy to see how a wife could be fed up. You told her the guy had tried and financial failure is no reason to leave a husband. You advised her to stick with the lummox because "Cary Grant is not waiting for you." For your information, Cary Grant has passed his sixtieth birthday, so it is possible that he, too, is "Oys-Gashpilt." You flubbed it, Annie.—*One Admirer Less*

Dear One: Age is only a number, and on him it looks good. At this writing Mr. Grant has had four marriages and an equal number of divorces so I am not betting one way or the other.

Dear Ann Landers: I have a friend who is a genius when it comes to chiseling small amounts. Whenever we get on a bus she says, "Put in my fare, Minnie. I haven't got change. I'll get it next time." When we go for coffee breaks I get stuck at least twice a week. Yesterday she asked me to pick up her watch at the jeweler's, neglecting to mention I'd have to pay $2.50 to get the watch out. I don't want to be petty, but I can't afford these small nicks. Help!—*Minnie The Mooched On*

Dear Min: No vocal chords, Minnie? Moochers must be dealt with in a skillful manner. Don't let her outfumble you. Develop an impediment in your reach. When you have coffee together don't be bashful about saying, "It's your turn. I got it yesterday." When she asks you to pick up items which have been repaired, you should assume they must be bailed out. Tell her, "Sorry, I can't afford it. Things are tough all over."

Dear Ann Landers: A friend of mine told me recently that when a husband dies, all the family debts, such as department store bills, time payments on appliances, cars, and house mortgages are automatically canceled, provided each account is under $450. I had never heard of this before. Please tell me if my friend has correct information?—*Learning Every Day*

Dear Learning: Your friend does not have correct information, and I hope you will set her straight. Women have been known to kill their husbands for less.

Dear Ann Landers: Several months ago a friend of mine had a nervous breakdown. When I told my husband about it, he said, "What did *she* have to worry about? She had a beautiful home, a nice husband, three swell kids, *and no job!*" Say something, will you? I'm—*Frothing*.

Dear Froth: The housewife is either the best-paid or the worst-paid woman in the world, depending on the man she's married to. If her husband is an ignorant, insensitive slob (like yours), she is the worst paid. If he is a thoughtful, understanding guy (like mine), she's the best paid.

Dear Ann Landers: Last year we loaned some money to friends. They promised to pay back $25 a month. We would not accept interest. For three months they paid the $25, then the payments stopped. Four months have gone by, and we haven't had so much as a phone call. Apparently they are ashamed to face us. It is sad that we have lost their friendship because we did them a favor. It is also sad that we are out several hundred dollars. How should such a request be handled in the future?—*Spilled Milk*

Dear Spilled: Don't make personal loans. Suggest that the loan be made from a bank. Offer to be a cosigner. You may still get stuck (as the cosigner), but your chances are infinitely better if the "reminders" come from a bank and not a friend.

Dear Ann Landers: My aunt gave our child a $25 check for confirmation. The check bounced. Stamped across the face of it was "Insufficient Funds." This aunt is well-to-do, and we can't understand why the check didn't clear. My husband says we should say nothing and let the matter drop. I don't agree. Would it be in bad taste to send the check back to my aunt? —*Dilemma*

Dear Dilemma: Put the check through a second time, with a note asking if the bank was in error. Banks are not infallible. If the check bounces a second time, forget it.

Dear Ann Landers: My spinster sister made a deathbed promise to Mamma that she would never be put in a nursing home. Without asking me, my sister said *I* would take her to live in my home. That was six years ago when Mamma was seventy-eight. Today she is eighty-four. Sister's promise was a safe one because no nursing home would take Mother. She belongs in a mental institution. Father left her a substantial inheritance from which she has been drawing interest for twenty-three years. Mother has not spent one dime of her own money since Father died. She is saving it "for her old age." My husband and I are going broke keeping nurses in our home around the clock. Mamma can't be left alone, and I haven't the strength to be with her more than eight hours a day. Even with a nurse on duty she has set fire to the mattress twice. She keeps saying she's going to leave all her money to a horse she sees on TV. It would not surprise me if she did. Please advise.—*Mary*

Dear Mary: It's senseless for you and your husband to go broke caring for Mother when she has an income of her own. Some people who put money away for a rainy day have to be told when it is raining. You need a lawyer.

Dear Ann Landers: George and I were married thirty-two years. We had a good life together. George owned a successful business and made good investments. He paid all the bills and gave me a cash allowance every two weeks. If I needed more money he gave it to me. George never talked to me about finances and I never asked any questions. Two weeks ago George had a cerebral hemorrhage in his office. He was unconscious when they brought him to the hospital. He died three days later. George's lawyer is a stranger to me. George's will was ten years old. For a smart man he left things in a terrible mess. He had stocks and bonds in vaults out of town, according to his former business partner, and now we are trying to find them. So I'd like to say to you women, don't let your husband "protect" you as mine did. Sit down with him and be realistic. Ask him, "If you died tomorrow, would your affairs be in the shape you want them to be in?" I wish I had.—*Daffodil*

Dear Daffodil: Reading your letter could be the most important thing thousands of women do today. Thank you for writing.

Dear Ann Landers: Fifteen years ago I lost my purse which had twenty dollars in it. My husband told me I was too dumb to handle money, and he hasn't given me a nickel since. I've never seen Walter's paycheck and have no idea what he earns. He keeps his bankbook in code. We have four children. They get a weekly allowance but I don't get one. Whenever I want a dollar I have to beg for it. Walter says he earns the money and is therefore entitled to dole it out as he sees fit. Is this right?—*On Charity*

Dear On: A wife who cares for the house and children doesn't need to bring home a paycheck. You are entitled to an allowance, and you can tell Mr. Great Heart I said so. It might be comforting for you to know that some women who have stacks of spending money are just as unhappy as you. Maybe unhappier. Read on.

Dear Ann Landers: American women love money, but they scream their heads off when their husbands do what is required to pay for the big home, the second car, vacations, and the better things in life. Business is murderously competitive. An executive needs eyes in the back of his head to see who is trying to knife him. Organizational footwork can leave a guy completely drained. So what happens? He comes home exhausted, and his wife considers it a personal insult if he doesn't become instantly aroused at the sight of her bending over the kitchen sink. If she should suggest something and he says he's too tired, she locks herself in the bathroom and cries for two hours. She is positive (a) he no longer loves her, (b) her life as a woman is finished, (c) he has another dame. Why is it that a woman has the born right to be too tired, but a man—*never!* So what happens to the husband who struggles to get ahead and isn't sure he's making it? His wife lets him know he isn't making it at home either, and he becomes doubly depressed. More conflict, more guilt, more anxiety, and finally total incapacitation. You won't print this letter, but I feel better for having written it. Now you can throw it on the floor, Babe. Thanks.—*Wall Street Warrior*

Dear Warrior: Your letter was too good for the floor. You make sense, boy. I liked it but the ladies whose letters follow didn't.

Dear Ann Landers: What a rotten trick you pulled on every love-starved wife in America. I wonder if you know how much trouble you cause. My Lochinvar has been giving me the old routine, "I'm dead tired beating my brains out making a living for you and the kids . . . bla-bla-bla." I've been saying it isn't normal for a man thirty-eight years old to be too tired for love no matter how hard he works. Then you come along with your lousy column and take *his* side. He has talked of nothing else for two days. Why don't you retire?—*Mad*

Dear Ann Landers: You are a traitor to your own sex. Why don't those big-money boys ask their wives which they would rather have, a second car or a second kiss? Wall Street Warrior said he was exhausted from "struggling to get ahead." I wonder if the money is as important to his wife as he thinks. And then he comes up with what is really bothering him—he is too tired! It was comforting to learn that there is *one* man

in the world who is too tired for sex. I wouldn't have
believed it. My first husband died when he was fifty,
and I think I know what killed him. My second husband was also after me night and day. I had to divorce
him to get some rest. Two years later I married a man
sixty-two, thinking I'd be out of danger. He's the worst
of the lot. I've heard you are a man and I'm beginning
to believe it.—*Gemini*

Dear Ann: I feel qualified to speak about the successful business or professional man who willingly
(perhaps eagerly) sacrifices his husband-father role in
exchange for the Big Buck. The excitement of the daily
battle on the money front is sufficient. They don't need
anything else in their lives. These men lack the true
understanding a successful husband-wife relationship
needs. If his woman becomes cold from waiting, or re-
sorts to a part-time replacement because she is lonely,
the Warrior couldn't care less. He is relieved that he
doesn't have to bother with her. The Warrior lives in a
world of work, and he adores it. Even his play must in
some way be related to his work. A wife and children
do not belong in this world. Anyone who cannot con-
tribute to his battle gains is relegated to the periphery.
No one will ever persuade me that a lack of interest in
the marriage bed stems from working too hard. This
bit of folklore was invented by a man who must have
known better. And anyone who regards this problem
as a problem of the rich had better think again. It exists at every economic level. The man who has spent
himself elsewhere and is tired when he comes home
got that way because he chose to. After years of loneliness and soul-searching ("Where did I fail?"), I confess that I wish I had married another kind of man. I
would gladly forgo my large home, the cars in the garage, my fine furs and jewelry, and the club member-

ships in exchange for a husband who will attend church with his family, show some interest in our children, and be available for the little confidences that can make marriage the special relationship that God intended it to be. Just sign me—*A Resident in Kenilworth*

Dear Ann Landers: You're probably fed up on letters from Wall Street Warriors and I don't mean to belabor the issue, but can a man from Cincinnati say something? I refer to the statement that hard-working husbands who spend themselves elsewhere and are too tired for romance got that way because they *chose* to. Please add, Ann Landers, that the same can be said of wives who spend themselves on the garden club, the Ladies Aid, the children, the laundry, and the housework. Years ago a clergyman's wife complained that her husband became romantic every Sunday night after his sermon had been delivered and the pressure was off. The wife said Sunday night didn't suit her because Monday morning was her hardest day. She had to get up early and do an enormous washing. Your advice was perfect. You told her to do her washing on Tuesdays. Please publish my letter. It contains a moral worth repeating.—*Chuck Who Loves You*

Dear Chuck: Here's your letter and I love you, too. Any reader who can come up with a line I wrote six years ago wins my undying devotion.

Dear Ann Landers: I married Ralph a year and a half ago. He is a fine guy who had been ditched by a gold digger. Two weeks before the wedding she drove out of his life in the new car he had given her as an engagement present. Ralph owes a balance of $350 on the new car. Now for the question: Ralph and I file our income tax jointly. We will soon be getting back about $375 from the government because we overpaid last year. Should I let Ralph take that money and pay off his obligation on the car? Most of the people I've asked feel I should be a good sport and give Ralph my half. But I don't want to be a sap. This obligation was incurred before I knew Ralph and I resent it.—*Ballerina*

Dear Bal: Help Ralph pay off the debt by kicking in your half of the refund check. What an ideal way to show him you are a Number One Number Two Girl.

Dear Ann Landers: Jack and I have been married fourteen years. We have six wonderful children. Jack's parents are people of means. They own a great deal of valuable real estate. The home we live in belongs to them, and we live here rent free. His parents even insist on paying the taxes. Jack's three brothers and their families also live in homes owned by their parents. My husband is an intelligent man, and I have great respect for his judgment. Yet his parents feel they must run our lives and even take over the disciplining of our children. Dozens of times I've wanted to tell my in-laws where to head in, but I've kept quiet for my husband's sake. I would give anything if we could live our own lives. But how?—*Loretta*

Dear Loretta: When you decide you want to lead your own lives so badly that you are willing to start paying rent, you will take the first step toward independence. Your in-laws feel justified in running your lives since they are keeping the roof over your heads. You'd be happier in a broom closet over a bowling alley. So move already. The next letter should be of special interest to you.

Dear Ann Landers: My husband is in business with his father, his brother, and his brother-in-law. Frequently my husband has bragged to friends that nothing is down on paper and there has never been anything in writing between them. There are no set salaries. Everybody takes what he needs. I'm not complaining, Ann, because we all live well. But I worry that one day this setup will lead to trouble. Last night I asked my husband what would happen if he died suddenly. He said his dad and brothers would always look after us and not to worry. When I suggested he get something in writing, he replied, "It would be an insult to my brothers." Is he right?—*Not Secure*

Dear Insecure: When combined, the three most explosive elements known to modern man are (a) money, (b) relatives, (c) nothing down on paper. Not only you, but the other wives, are entitled to a legal document making provisions for the family of a partner who dies. Get together with the other women and insist that your husbands see a lawyer. It probably has been on *their* minds, too.

Dear Ann Landers: John and I have been married six years. We have three children. John's parents live two blocks from us. They are good people, not the interfering type, and we all get along fine. The problem is they have few friends and no interests other than our family. Their lives are centered around us and our children. John's company wants him to go to another state as district manager. It would mean a big promotion and a substantial salary increase. My father-in-law says if John will pass it up and remain here, he will make up the financial difference. He says money isn't everything and their lives will be empty without us. Comment please.—*Alice*

Dear Alice: There's something involved here that is much more important than money. Like independence. Parents should not ask a married son to pass up a promotion because they want him and his family in town.

Dear Ann Landers: It's easy for you to sit there and give advice. I often wonder how much of your advice you follow. Several weeks ago you told a woman whose husband had a better job offer that they should move, even if it meant depriving his parents of the pleasure of their company. How much moving around have *you* done?—*Mrs. Nosy*

Dear Mrs.: Our van log looks like this: From Sioux City, Iowa, to St. Louis. From St. Louis back to Sioux City and on to Little Rock. From Little Rock to New Orleans. From New Orleans to Milwaukee. From Milwaukee to Los Angeles. From Los Angeles to Chicago. From Chicago to Eau Claire, Wisconsin. From Eau Claire back to Chicago, where we have lived since 1955—the longest stretch in twenty-nine years of marriage. Any more questions?

Dear Ann Landers: I could kiss you for telling the world that some wives handle the pocketbook better than their husbands. We've had the problem in our family for years. After my husband read that column he said, "OK, I'll hand over my check beginning with the next one." He had to agree I couldn't do worse than he has done. Thanks for helping me win a battle I've been fighting for fourteen years! You've got a pretty smart head on those forty-eight-year-old shoulders, Ann. Thank you for what you've done for me.— *Heading For The Black*

Dear Heading: I'm glad I helped. And now, to keep the record straight, the head is resting on fifty-year-old shoulders. I added a couple—while you weren't looking.

Dear Ann Landers: A fellow who works in this office took a girl to a church bazaar. He paid $1 each for their bingo cards. The jumbo jackpot was $200.

The girl won. When they dumped the money in front of her she handed the fellow a dollar and said, "Gee, thanks. This must be my lucky night." He was burned up. The office force has mixed feelings. Was the fellow entitled to all the money, half the money, or none of the money?—*Reserving Judgment.*

Dear Judge: The division of potential winnings should have been settled in advance. A good arrangement would have been a 50–50 split in the event either of them won. If that greedy girl cared for the fellow, she lost a great deal more than she won.

Dear Ann Landers: My husband and I have been playing bridge with a certain couple for over twelve years. They are superb bridge players and we are, too. We have a game every Thursday night, and when we play cards we mean business. It is not uncommon for $40 or $50 to change hands in an evening. A few days ago I learned that this couple had an elegant dinner party at their club. More than thirty couples were present. My husband and I were not invited. I am deeply hurt. Shall I tell them at our next card game that if we aren't good enough to be invited to their parties, we aren't good enough to play cards with them?—*Grand Slam*

Dear Grand: The answer is in your letter. You said, "When we play cards we mean business." Well, *they* mean business, too, and that's the nature of your relationship. If you enjoy matching skills with this couple, continue to play cards with them, but recognize the fact that you are not social friends.

Dear Ann Landers: Why do people who are loaded with money always win the door prizes, the raffles, and everything else there is to win? It happened again last night. My husband and I attended a church bazaar.

When they drew the name of the winner of the mink stole, it was a woman who had a mink scarf on her shoulders and a mink coat at home. Everyone must have thought (as I did) that it would have been very nice if she had turned the stole back and let them auction it off again. Of course, she didn't. They never do. What do you think about this?—*Bystander*

Dear By: The rich don't always win. It just seems like it. And, of course, everyone notices because they *are* rich. Yes, it would have been nice if Mrs. Gotrocks had turned back the prize, but she was under no obligation to do so.

Dear Ann Landers: Our daughter, Grace, is twenty-three years old. We've given her voice lessons, piano, four years at a fine university, a trip to Europe, and plenty of love. Grace has an excellent job. She earns $400 a month. We don't ask for room and board. We only ask that she stop charging everything to us. As a college graduation gift we bought her a new car. Whenever I ask Grace to drive me somewhere she gets a pained look on her face. Yesterday she said, "How did you get to the doctor's office before I had a car?" Grace wants her own apartment but she says we should pay the rent. Frankly my nerves need a rest, and I'd be happy if she moved out. Please help me find the right words.—*Tired*

Dear Tired: You've found the right words, but you are telling them to the wrong person. Grace is spoiled rotten. She is also an expert at mooching, which should come as no surprise. She's been practicing since childhood. Tell her to find an apartment. If she can't manage the rent, suggest she get a roommate. Too bad Grace and Regina, the subject of the next letter, live on opposite coasts. It would be lovely if they could get together.

Dear Ann Landers: Our niece who is only twenty-seven lost her young husband in a tragic accident six months ago. Her parents felt Regina would be better off in another city, away from memories, so they asked if she could live with me until she found a job and an apartment of her own. Regina has been with us four months. She found an excellent position as a bilingual secretary at $125 a week and seems to have recovered from her grief. She has a date almost every night. The girl says nothing about finding her own apartment. In the meantime I do her washing and ironing and I prepare her meals. She entertains in our home and hands me a grocery list for her parties. She has never offered to pay for anything, says she wouldn't insult us by suggesting our hospitality is purchasable. We are pleased that Regina feels at home here, but we think she should start to pay for room and board. On the other hand, she has suffered a great tragedy and we feel sorry for her. Advise us please.—*Just Folks*

Dear Folks: If Regina is dating every night, she has recovered. Suggest that she "insult" you with about thirty dollars a week until she finds a place of her own, which I hope will be soon. In case you think this is a "girl" type problem, read on.

Dear Ann Landers: Our twenty-year-old son was lucky and landed a good job close to home after he graduated from high school two years ago. His take-home pay is $97 a week. I am happy to have him home but it is strictly his idea—not mine. I do his laundry, fix him a hearty breakfast every morning, and he rarely misses supper with the family. I've hinted that I could use a few dollars (there are four younger children), but he ignored the remark. Should I come right out and ask him to pay room and board or would this be greedy?—*Missouri Mom*

Dear Mom: Since Missouri is the "Show Me" state, I suggest your son show you about 25 percent of his paycheck. This is the Ann Landers' formula for unmarried kids who live at home and enjoy all the comforts of their childhood. So, stop hinting, Mom. Tell him.

Dear Ann Landers: I didn't like your answer to "Crisis In Suburbia." A mother wanted to know if her sons were entitled to an increase in allowance because their father received a promotion and a pay raise. You said, "Yes, provided they take on extra chores and *earn* the increase." I am a grandfather who is appalled at what is happening to the younger generation. I think it's disgraceful to pay children for doing what they *should* do. After all they are a part of the family, so why shouldn't they pitch in? Paying children for every little thing makes me sick. I say kids should help around the house because they live in the house and eat and sleep there. That's reason enough.—*Three Score And Ten*

Dear Three Score: Sorry, but the days are gone when you can give a kid a nickel and say, "Go have a good time." Children ought to have a little money to spend and to save. Most kids today get an allowance for tying up the bathroom and hogging the telephone. I'm in favor of teaching children the relationship between work and rewards. This can best be achieved by assigning specific chores and making it clear that the allowance is payment.

Dear Ann Landers: What is this world coming to, anyway? My husband received an insulting letter today from a reputable jewelry store. It is outrageous that a place of business would go to such extremes to collect a bill. First let me tell you we are respectable people and we try to pay our obligations on time. Once in a while we get behind, but we've never gone completely dead on a bill. Here is the letter we received. Please comment. "Dear Sir: Your account has been on our books for over a year. We respectfully remind you that we have now carried you longer than your mother did. Thank you for your prompt attention." Isn't that awful?—*Disgusted With Gimmicks*

Dear Disgusted: Sorry, but I think it's pretty funny. It ill behooves a person who is a year in arrears to criticize a merchant who tries to get his money.

Dear Ann Landers: Please educate a lot of kids who have the wrong idea. Just because my dad works in a bank everyone expects me to be rich. The kids seem to think that people who work in banks can help themselves to money, just like people who work in a fruit market can pinch off a few grapes or eat an apple whenever they feel like it. Yesterday I was at a scout meeting and we were short $5.70 for the picnic budget. One of the kids said, "Mel can get the money from his dad's bank." So please, Ann Landers, tell everybody that bank employees get a paycheck like schoolteachers and truck drivers, and sometimes the check isn't very big. The money in the bank belongs to the depositors, and it had better not be missing. Thank you.—*Mel*

Dear Mel: Here's your letter and I think you told 'em better than I could. In case the kids don't know it maybe we'd better mention the bank examiners who come around every so often and check the books and count the money. If things don't add up right, somebody could go to jail.

Dear Ann Landers: I have been going steady with a very nice man for two years. We are both single and in our mid-thirties. Two months ago Jack borrowed ten dollars from me. He hasn't called me since. I'd be very happy to forget about the ten dollars and consider it a gift. Last week I telephoned Jack twice to talk things over. Both times he was very rude and seemed in a hurry to get off the phone. Jack's birthday is next month, and Easter is coming up. We always celebrated these occasions together. Shall I mail him a card or a friendly note or perhaps a little gift? I want to send him something. What do you suggest?—*Sudden Jolt*

Dear Jolt: Send him a bill—and forget the creep.

Dear Ann Landers: Chain letters are driving me out of my mind. Years ago it was a sweet little good-luck poem from a friend. Now it has become a pain in the ankle. In the past two weeks I have received five chain letters—all from strangers. Yesterday I received a chain letter instructing me to make eight copies and send each along with a pint of bourbon to the last person on the list. This morning I received a chain letter instructing me to send five dollars to the last name on the list and get five copies out within twenty-four hours or I would have some very bad luck. I confess I was afraid not to follow the instructions because I am a superstitious person, so I sent the bourbon and the money and the copies as requested. Now I am mad at myself for being a sucker. Please tell me if you have ever heard of anyone who made anything off of these crazy chain letters.—*Chicken*

Dear Chick: Chain letters involving anything of value are illegal. They are also stupid. No, I have never heard of anyone who profited from a chain letter other than the people who got your five dollars and your bourbon.

Dear Ann Landers: Last week I got on the bus and discovered I had no change. I didn't have any folding money in my wallet either, which was embarrassing. The driver smiled and said, "OK. Next time, Buddy." It dawned on me that this was the third time in three weeks I had been caught without change. Last night the mystery was solved. Half an hour after my wife and I retired, she crept out of bed, and with the help of a flashlight she emptied my pockets. I give her a generous allowance, and there is no reason for her to do this. Is she playing a childish game or what? I haven't said anything because I don't know what to make of it. What goes—besides my change, that is?— *Big Daddy*

Dear Daddy: Sounds as if the lady has a bat in her belfry. Tonight empty your pockets and place the contents on the dresser with a note, asking her to please leave you enough money for bus fare. And P.S.: Keep a couple of quarters in your shoe, just in case.

Dear Ann Landers: My husband thinks nothing of spending $200 on fishing equipment or $175 on a camera, but he will slit a tube of toothpaste down the middle with a razor blade to make sure he gets every last ounce of toothpaste. This man is a busy executive. When I see him spending time in the morning performing this penny-ante trick, it irritates me. Can you explain this?—*Mrs. Skinflint*

Dear Mrs. Flint: Your husband happens to be tight about toothpaste. President Johnson used to go around the White House turning out lights. We all have our secret little miser stunts. Even you, I'll bet.

Ten

YOU CAN'T TELL A KID BY HIS AGE

My daily mail presents irrefutable evidence that an astonishing number of financial and professional giants are in many respects emotional midgets. Merely because a man has replaced his thumb with a cigar is not proof that he is grown up. And the woman who teaches philosophy at Stanford may be so emotionally chained to her mother that hubby is about to give her the heave-ho—Ph.D. and all.

Maturity, according to the *World Book Dictionary,* is "to be fully developed in body and mind—the condition of having achieved complete excellence." Do you know an individual who fits this description? I do not. Such a person does not exist. No mind can be fully developed. Moreover, complete excellence, like total happiness and perfect beauty, are figments of the imagination or, at best, in the eye of the beholder.

Each of us possesses large (or small) pockets of immaturity. Witness the brilliant attorney who cannot free himself from a domineering mother, the middle-aged wife who still wants to be Daddy's girl, the teenager, first in his class at Princeton who drives 110 miles an hour when his girl dumps him for a Rutgers man, the compulsive eater to whom food is a substitute for love, the eternal Don Juan who jumps from bed to bed to reassure himself of his masculinity.

Frequently when I am asked how to deal with an

immature sweetheart, teen, husband, or wife, I say, "Tell him to grow up!" Good advice, but not practical. One does not grow up merely because he is told to do so. Emotional growth, like physical growth, occurs one day at a time.

Maturity, then, is the ability to handle frustration, control anger, and settle differences without violence or destruction.

Maturity is patience. It is the willingness to postpone gratification, to pass up the immediate pleasure or profit in favor of the long-term gain.

Maturity is perseverance, sweating out a project or a situation in spite of opposition and discouraging setbacks.

Maturity is unselfishness, responding to the needs of others.

Maturity is the capacity to face unpleasantness and disappointment without becoming bitter.

Maturity is the gift of remaining calm in the face of chaos. This means peace, not only for ourselves, but for those with whom we live and for those whose lives touch ours.

Maturity is the ability to disagree without being disagreeable.

Maturity is humility. A mature person is able to say, "I was wrong." He is also able to say, "I am sorry." And when he is proven right, he does not have to say, "I told you so."

Maturity is the ability to make a decision, to act on that decision, and to accept full responsibility for the outcome.

Maturity means dependability, integrity, keeping one's word. The immature have excuses for everything. They are the chronically tardy, the no-shows, the gutless wonders who fold in the crises. Their lives are a maze of broken promises, unfinished business, and former friends.

Maturity is the ability to live in peace with that which we cannot change.

————————

Do you recognize anyone you know in the letters that follow?

Dear Ann Landers: I am writing this letter on my honeymoon. Ev and I checked into this motel after a beautiful church wedding. Ev looked around the room for the TV, and when he didn't see one he went to the room clerk. He was told that some of the TV sets were being repaired and there was a shortage. Ev said, "You advertise a TV set in every room and I want one." The room clerk replied, "I figured honeymooners would miss TV less than other folks, but maybe I was wrong in your case." Ev reached over to hit him and one of the bellboys pulled him off. I pleaded with Ev to come to the room so I could talk to him. He said, "No, I'm going to sit in this lobby until I get a TV set." Ev sat in the lobby until 3:30 A.M. and I cried all night. What do I do now?—*Untouched Bride*

Dear Bride: As I said in my telegram, if Ev is still sitting in the lobby when this message arrives, take a train, plane, or bus and go home. The groom needs professional help. He used the TV gambit as an excuse to avoid the role of a husband. If Ev refuses to get the help he needs, speak to your clergyman and a lawyer about an annulment.

Dear Ann Landers: Why has no one labeled the husband's hazardous and nerve-shredding driving for what it is—the twentieth-century version of wife-beating? I'd like to describe a daily drama, and I hope the players recognize themselves before the lids finally come down on their caskets. A couple goes for a drive. The outing becomes an occasion for the husband to act out all his hostilities and aggressions. Once behind the wheel he seizes the opportunity to get even with his wife for every rotten thing she has ever said to him, real or imagined. Risky driving has become a socially acceptable technique for punishing a wife for whatever is wrong in a man's life. Maybe he hates his mother or his boss or his job or, more often than not, his own inadequacies could be making him miserable. But it's the wife who catches the brunt of it every time. I suggest that couples who are constantly at war because of the husband's driving find out what is really bothering him and settle the problem at home.—*A Survivor*

Dear Survivor: The experts in the field of traffic safety tell us that an important factor in many serious accidents is hostility. Sometimes the anger is directed at the world in general, or it may be aimed at the wife-passenger, as you suggest. There's also the possibility that the wild driver may have a subconscious desire to kill himself. People who are mad at their relatives or the world or themselves should stay at home and hammer away at a punching bag or take the bus to a gym and play handball.

Dear Ann Landers: My husband is forty. We have three children. Every evening my husband races the kids to the bathtub and uses all the hot water. I wouldn't swear to it, but I think he also floats the baby's rubber duck. When the kids take their baths, I have to heat water on the stove and carry it upstairs. I have asked my husband to be more considerate but he just sits there and sulks. Have you a solution?—*Water-logged*

Dear Logged: You need a larger water heater, and you need it now. A forty-year-old man who is still playing with a rubber duck is not likely to approach this problem in a mature manner, so work it out alone.

Dear Ann Landers: What can I do about a boyfriend whose chief interest in life is food? Sidney is not a teen-ager. He is twenty-four and about thirty pounds overweight. He never holds my hand in a movie because he is eating popcorn. At football games while other couples hold hands Sidney must have his hands free for the potato chips. Even when he drives, one hand is in a bag of jelly beans. The other evening while we were watching TV Sidney munched litchi nuts until I thought I'd lose my mind. When I saw him to the door he said, "I'd kiss you good night but my teeth are stuck together on account of the taffy." I could compete with other females, Ann, but how does a girl compete with food?—*Tina*

Dear Tina: A twenty-four-year-old man who can't kiss his girl good night because his teeth are stuck together with taffy should see a head doctor.

Dear Ann Landers: Mom and Dad fight like cats and dogs. I wish I had a dollar for every time we kids had to separate them and beg them to stop yelling so we could get some sleep. Dad's favorite gag is to take embarrassing pictures of Mom and pass them around to friends when they go to a party. Once he caught a picture of her while she was asleep, with her mouth open. Another time he took a picture of her washing the kitchen floor in an old bathing suit and tennis shoes. Last week Mom put a rubber snake in the medicine chest, and when Dad opened up the chest, the snake popped out and he darned near had a heart attack. There are five kids in our family, and we are raising each other. In case you haven't guessed, they both drink a lot. Can you help them straighten around?—*The Five J.'s*

Dear J.: Your parents need more help than I can give them. You kids could profit from Alateen. This organization is for children who must live with alcoholism. Write to Al-Anon Family Group Headquarters, Inc., P.O. Box 182, Madison Square Station, New York, N.Y. 10010.

Dear Ann Landers: My husband retired last year at the age of sixty-five. If he had worked half as hard at his job as he is working on his hobbies, we would be millionaires. Four months ago Clyde bought a second-hand cello. He takes two lessons a week and practices three hours every day. I don't even care for *good* cello music so you can imagine what I go through listening to Clyde practice. When our children were young somebody in the house was always practicing something but it didn't bother me nearly so much as this. Any suggestions?—*Had It*

Dear It: Don't complain because your sixty-five-year-old husband is fiddling around. At least *he* has a cello. Get a transistor radio and carry it from room to room when you do your housework.

Dear Ann Landers: Eight months ago when I started to work as a volunteer in a hospital I met a very attractive patient. Jim had been seriously injured in a motorcycle accident. He was in the hospital for nearly six months. I saw him at least four times a week. The day Jim was discharged he asked me to marry him and I said Yes. He bought me a ring the following week. The very first day he was allowed to leave the house he took his motorcycle out and got into another accident. He almost lost a leg. The first thing he asked when he came out of the anesthetic was how badly was his bike damaged. Today when I took him out in the wheelchair all he talked about was getting a new motorcycle. I love this guy, but I don't want to be a widow at twenty-two. Do I have the right to tell him I will marry him only if he gives up the motorcycle?—*Maurine*

Dear M.: You do—and you should. I also suggest that you learn what other accidents Jim has had. I suspect there have been several. Find out from an authority what this means before you tie up with him forever.

Dear Ann Landers: I am sick to death of reading articles titled "Who Is Boss in Your Family?" "The Lady Wears the Pants," or "What Has Happened to Man's Role in Society?" Please tell me what a wife can do when her husband refuses to behave like a grownup man. Somebody in the family must make decisions, and my husband simply won't do it. He is lethargic and indecisive. If a bill doesn't get paid, he couldn't care less. The house has been falling apart for two years, and he hasn't even noticed. Although he is a carpenter, he refuses to pick up a hammer around here. I have to hire a man to make the repairs or I make them myself. The only thing my husband does with no prodding is drink. He is gassed every weekend.
—*Married To A Grown-Up Baby*

Dear Married: People find each other for a reason. Now you know why he found you. Or did you find *him,* the doll? Wives who are movers and shakers were aggressive before marriage. They intentionally selected a man who needed to be moved and shaken, or they let such a man select them. Now do you get it?

Dear Ann: Last October our seventeen-year-old son asked his father and me to sign papers so he could be married. We agreed because his girl friend was four months' pregnant. Her parents came over with their minister and an uncle who is a prizefighter. The marriage lasted four months. My husband had to pay for the divorce, which he did happily because he couldn't stand the sight of the girl. Last week the boy asked us to sign more papers because he has met another girl he would like to marry. This girl is not in a family way, but she is twenty-three years old and has two children by a former marriage. Our son swears he knows what he is doing this time and is begging us to let him prove it. What should we do?—*Gray For A Reason*

Dear Gray: Your son is seventeen years of age. He already has a marriage, a child, and a divorce, and now he wants to get married again. And you are asking me whether or not to let him??!! The answer is *no!* Your son is not ready for marriage, and if you sign those papers you'd better start saving your money for another divorce.

Dear Ann: I wrote to you recently about the problems I was having with my husband. You suggested we see a licensed marriage counselor. Yesterday was our third visit. When we left the marriage counselor's office, my husband was in a surly mood and said he didn't feel like driving. He ordered me to take the wheel. I was feeling punk and told him I'd rather not drive. He got in the driver's seat, gunned the motor, and raced down the highway at eighty miles an hour, reading the newspaper at the same time. I informed him he was behaving childishly and I was shocked that he would risk my life as well as his own just to prove I'd better give him his way or suffer the consequences. Now we aren't speaking. Was I wrong to refuse to drive?—*Mixed Up*

Dear Mixed: Did you need this incident as proof that your husband is grossly immature? You should have anticipated his petulant and punitive behavior and taken the wheel no matter how punk you felt. Better to arrive home ill than dead.

Dear Ann Landers: My wife is always shoving your column under my nose, especially when you have a letter about a husband who likes to drink beer and sit in front of the TV. Please print this letter so I can shove a column under *her* nose for a change. We have four fine sons—the oldest twelve, the youngest seven. Whenever one of them has a fight with a neighborhood kid, my wife jumps right in, phoning mothers and going over in person "to make sure our boy comes out all right." The kids always patch up their quarrels, but my wife is not on speaking terms with half the neighborhood.—*The Old Man*

Dear Man: A mother who becomes involved in the petty squabbles of her children is more childish than they. Ask your wife to please wait until you get home before she "does anything." By then the trouble will have been settled—by the kids.

Dear Ann: My in-laws are both seventy-three. My husband and I have dinner with them every week. For the past several months my father-in-law has not been acting very fatherly. He never does anything out of the way in the presence of his wife or my husband. He manages to get me in the kitchen or in the back hall. When I was dating I knew how to deal with characters who sneaked up and planted an unwanted kiss on the back of my neck. I belted them one and I never had any trouble after that. What should I do in this case? If my husband knew he'd be wild.—*Disgusted*

Dear D.: You can't belt a seventy-three-year-old man, particularly a father-in-law. Call on your sense of humor to save the day. Nickname him "Old Love In Bloom" and keep it loud and funny—and out in the open.

Dear Ann: Bob is twenty-seven. I am twenty-four. We have been married two years and expect our first child any minute. Last night Bob's older sister telephoned to say her daughter Barbara, aged seventeen, was in tears. Barbara's date broke his leg and couldn't take her to an important high-school dance. She asked Bob if he'd be a lifesaver and take Barbara. He replied, "I'd love to." I don't feel a married man has any business at a high-school dance. Furthermore, this is no time for him to leave me alone. He says I am narrow-minded and jealous. If you tell me I am wrong, I will apologize.—*P.G. Wife*

Dear Wife: Your husband belongs at a high-school dance like a skunk belongs at a lawn party. If he goes, I hope the stork drops the bundle while he is out bugalooing with the kids. It would serve him right.

Dear Ann Landers: Millie and I have been married for three years. She was always a mamma's girl, but I thought she'd grow up when we moved out of town. In fact, I asked for a transfer so I could get her four hundred miles away from her mother. Every night Millie is on the phone crying about some darned fool thing. Either she laundered blue socks with the white tablecloth or her cake caved in. Tonight she was bawling because she fell off her bicycle and twisted her knee. What can I do?—*Puzzled*

Dear Puz: I hope Millie has been crying after 6 P.M. —it's cheaper. A married woman who continues to lean on her mother may not be getting the proper emotional support from her husband. I suggest counseling for you both.

Dear Ann Landers: My mother and father were happily married for fifty-two years. Mother passed away last June. Dad took it awfully hard—for about three weeks. Now he is so busy making dates with the widows in the neighborhood we don't know where he is half the time. Dad used to complain that his teeth didn't fit and his lumbago was bothering him. But since he has become a ladies' man he says he feels better than he has in years. To look at him you'd never guess he's seventy-five. All this is fine, but I'm worried that the night life might kill him. Is it possible that he is in his second childhood?—*Concerned*

Dear Con: Leave him alone. His second childhood may be more fun than his first. If he drops dead at seventy-five kissing a widow that's not a bad way to go.

Dear Ann: Please tell me what to do about a husband who breaks things in anger. Never *his* things, mind you. Only my things. Immediately after he destroyed my best hand mirror (a gift from my mother), he ripped up a book I was reading and screamed, "There—I hope you are satisfied. You've been asking for this all day." I am sick and tired of being blamed for this lunatic's destructiveness. He has been behaving this way ever since we were married (ten years ago). Our children don't understand their father's violent outbursts, and they become frightened when he goes on these wild rampages. What is wrong with him and what can I do about it?—*Hutchinson Heartache*

Dear Hutch: A California psychiatrist wrote a book called *Games People Play*. Your husband is playing a game called "See What You Made Me Do?" "See What You Made Me Do?" is played by an individual who is mad at himself. He yearns for an excuse to be mad at someone else. So he behaves in an outrageous manner and blames the first person who walks through the door. The only known cure for such childishness is to grow up.

Dear Ann Landers: My age: thirty-six. Background: Married twice. First marriage to a man twice my age. (I was sixteen.) My mother pushed me into it because

she thought he was rich. I said OK because I thought
he was kind. We were both wrong. The third time he
broke my nose, I divorced him. My second marriage
lasted two years. My husband drank vodka martinis
for breakfast with beer chasers. He worked for the city
and had a fatal accident at work. I'm sure he was
smashed on the job, but they paid off nicely, and I got
a generous settlement. I bought a small café three
years ago and have been doing very well. The problem: A nineteen-year-old applied for a job four
months ago, and I hired him. He is handsome, hard-
working, and I think we are in love. He is very
grown-up for his age and looks a lot older than he is.
The Army wouldn't take him because he has a steel
plate in his head. He wants to marry me. What do you
think?—*Angie*

Dear Angie: The kid has a steel plate in his head.
What's *your* excuse? A fellow nineteen should be looking for a girl seventeen. If you are smart, you'll help
him find one. Where's his mother, anyway?

Dear Ann Landers: Apparently you were not aware
of the changes in the Social Security laws or you would
have given better advice to that seventy-year-old
widow who moved in with a gentleman of the same
age. The woman said marriage was out because she
would then lose her deceased husband's Social Security. A widow can now remarry and collect 50 percent
of her deceased husband's Social Security. Please tell
her—and thousands of others.—*Field Representative
F.N.T.*

Dear Rep: Thank you for the information. And now
to all of you golden-age swingers who are living together without benefit of clergy, check with your local
Social Security office and get married already.

Eleven

KEEPING YOUR COOL

Seventy-eight years before Christ was born, Cicero said, "A perverse temper and a fretful disposition will make any state of life whatsoever unhappy."

Much of the unhappiness I hear about stems from a fretful disposition or a perverse temper. Since it is humanly impossible to be cheerful, charming, and agreeable from dawn to dusk, one must expect misunderstandings, irritability, and problems.

The best way to resolve problems is by talking them out. Boiling in silence can build an ulcer. Furthermore, nothing is so infuriating as the mate who "refuses to discuss it"—and sits there like a clam with a broken hinge.

A good marriage can tolerate differences in opinion. When two people agree on everything, their marriage is either a dictatorship or a bore. Honest verbalization is essential to a good relationship. But an important distinction exists between honest verbalization and verbal assault and battery.

Frank talk can mean a battle, and this is not always bad. Battle can be useful, honorable, and even noble. All married couples should learn the art of battle as they should learn the art of making love. Good battle is objective and honest—never vicious or cruel. Good battle is healthy and constructive, and brings to a marriage the principle of equal partnership.

Time and place are of utmost importance. No problem was ever solved before breakfast, or the moment a husband gets home from work. And it goes without saying that a battle should be a private affair. Every social circle has at least one couple notorious for slugging it out in public. The husband or wife who attempts to gain support by launching his attack in the presence of family and friends succeeds only in generating sympathy for his spouse.

Profanity, shouting, and destructive words are weapons of a loser. Physical violence is, of course, unspeakable. Hitting and slapping is a child's way of relieving anger and frustration. A grownup who behaves in this immature manner needs professional help.

Anger is a normal emotion. It is nothing to be ashamed of. Indeed, we should be ashamed if we are so indifferent to what is happening around us that we do not at times become outraged. But the mature individual expresses his anger in socially acceptable ways. He keeps his cool. No one has the right to destroy property or to infringe on the rights of others, no matter how noble his cause. There is much in our society that needs change, and it is the angry citizen who expresses his anger in a responsible, constructive manner who will make this a better world for all people.

———————

Dear Ann Landers: I'm at the end of my rope with this lunkhead I'm married to. What would you do if on the day before your birthday your husband handed you a quarter and said, "Here, honey, go buy yourself a birthday card"?—*Counting to 100*

Dear Counting: I would take the quarter, smile tenderly, thank him for his thoughtfulness, and tell him he was sweet to remember. I would then buy a card for ten cents and bring the last of the big spenders fifteen cents in change.

Dear Ann Landers: I took the advice you gave Counting To 100, and now I have a lot more trouble than I need. My birthday was Sunday and my husband, Jake, who also reads your column, handed me a quarter and said, "Here, honey, go buy yourself a card." I did like you said, Ann; I bought myself a card for a dime. When Jake came home for dinner I said, "Thanks for the birthday present. I found exactly what I wanted for ten cents. Here is your change." I now have a loose tooth in front and my left eye is swollen shut. I'd appreciate it if you'd lay off the smart-mouth answers.—*Also Counting*

Dear Also: Does your husband have a kid brother running around loose? Read the next letter.

Dear Ann Landers: I didn't go to a family reunion tonight because I can hardly see out of one eye. Yesterday my boyfriend hit me. I am seventeen, and my boyfriend is eighteen. I really dig him the most, and he is groovy in lots of ways, but he has a bad temper. We got into a dumb argument over nothing, and I jokingly said, "You are stupid!" Suddenly he hauled off and socked me. I must say he was awfully nice about it right after. He went and got me a washcloth and some ice. He has hit me a couple of times before, but this is the first time he has ever given me a black eye. If my folks knew about it they would make me stop seeing him, and I would die of loneliness. Is there any way I can get him to control his temper?—*Bonnie*

Dear Bonnie: Give Clyde the air, unless of course, you enjoy shiners and maybe a fractured jaw one of these days.

Dear Ann Landers: Whenever my mother is in the car and I am driving, she bugs me until I am ready to flip out. It's "Watch out for those kids, Billy. You're awfully close to that car ahead, Billy! The fellow behind you is going to pass you, Billy. You're going too fast. Use those mirrors. Watch that light!" I've been driving for two years and I've never had an accident, a ticket, or even a warning. I am a much better driver than my mother, and most of my friends are better drivers than *their* mothers, but we all get bugged just the same. I beg you to say something in your column about this, Ann Landers. Think back to when you were a teen-ager—or did they have cars in those days? —*Flint, Mich.*

Dear Flint: That last line is not likely to get me on your side, kid, but I'll happily say a word in behalf of teen-agers who have good safety records. A yelling mother can destroy the confidence of a teen-age driver. Moreover it is dangerously distracting to have someone barking orders. Please, mothers, remember that Junior is out of rompers. His eyes and reflexes are probably better than yours.

Dear Ann Landers: I read that letter about the husband who was dressed up in his good suit and asked his wife to change the tire because she was in jeans. Your answer was terrible. If that had been my wife, I would have given her a swift kick in the Levis and left her with the car and the flat tire to figure things out for herself. It makes me mad the way women today want to drive buses, trucks, and taxis, fly airplanes, be lawyers and doctors, and run for public office, but they don't want to do any of the hard work connected with the job. I say nobody should get behind the wheel of a car if he isn't willing to change a tire. I work in a post office that has hired several women in the past few years. These women get the same pay as men, but they don't go near the eighty-pound sacks because a law says they don't have to pick up anything heavier than forty pounds. Is this fair?—*Feduplentywithem*

Dear Fed: Kwitcherbellyachin. The law you are

complaining about doesn't exist. According to the U.S. Post Office in Chicago, people are hired if they are qualified to do the job. The sex of the applicant is not a consideration. The female carriers in Chicago lug eighty-pound sacks and work just as hard as the men.

Dear Ann Landers: Aunt Jennie has many good qualities and the children love her, but she makes me so mad at times I could chew nails. Our four sons (between six and twelve years of age) are full of pep and they get into everything. Anyone who has raised children knows growing boys fall down, cut themselves, break teeth and occasionally arms and legs. Whenever Aunt Jennie hears that one of the boys has had an accident, she asks my husband, "Where was their mother when it happened?" He turns to me and says, "That's a good question. Where *were* you?" I resent the implication that I am derelict in my duty. How can I defend myself?—*Irritated*

Dear Irritated: You don't need to defend yourself. Things happen to kids even when their mothers are present. The next time Aunt Jennie asks, "Where was their mother when it happened?" tell her you were dead drunk in a beer parlor—as usual. That should melt her bridgework.

Dear Ann Landers: As a nondrinker who once had a terrible problem I used to dread being pressured by friends and acquaintances to "have just one." Now I look forward to it. It goes like this:

Persistent Party: "Have a drink, Joe."

Me: "No, thanks."

Persistent Party: "Don't be a wet blanket, Joe. Have a drink."

Me: "I'd rather not."

Persistent Party: "Oh, c'mon, Joe. Have a drink. It'll do you good. You look like you need a lift."

Me: "OK. You win."

I take the drink, open the pest's suit coat pocket, and pour in the drink. If it's a lady, the drink goes down her front. I then stuff the glass in his pocket or her bra and turn to speak with someone else. Funny how the word gets around the room, and fewer and fewer people try to get me to take a drink anymore.—*Just Plain Joe*

Dear Joe: Your approach is novel but I have two questions: 1. How many of your own teeth do you have left? 2. How many parties have you been invited to lately?

Dear Ann Landers: I read the letter from Joe, a nondrinker who got fed up with people who tried to force liquor on him at cocktail parties. His solution, pouring the drink into the nagger's pocket, was a gutsy one, but he was justified. People must protect themselves against boors as best they can. Now, what can dieters do when the hostess keeps pushing food on them? One friend said to me last night, "Oh, I fixed the spaghetti and garlic bread just for you." (That's three pounds right there.) Another friend always pleads, "Just taste it." Then she shoves a corn fritter under my nose. Of course, my resistance breaks down and I eat all the things I shouldn't. Is there a solution?—*Bigger Than Both of Us*

Dear Bigger: Yes. Eat at home and tell your friends, "Doctor's orders." People who accept dinner invitations are expected to eat what is served, unless they have forewarned the hostess.

Dear Ann Landers: I have an aunt who is very fat. She is also very rich. Her husband owns half the lumber in North Carolina. This fat aunt came to visit a few days ago. I know it was dumb, but I accidentally left my ukulele on a chair in the living room. Well, this fat aunt goes and sits right down on my uke and smashes it to smithereens. She didn't say one word about buying me a new uke. All she could talk about was how kids today don't take care of their things and how the crashing sound of that uke almost gave her heart failure. I think it was mighty cheap of my aunt not to offer to buy me a new uke. She could buy me a whole store full of ukes and not miss the money.— *Former Owner Of A Ukulele*

Dear Former Owner: You should not have left the uke on the chair, but people should pay attention to where they sit, too. She might have sat on a darning needle, scissors, or a small child. This column appears in many cities in North Carolina. Let's hope Auntie sees your letter and comes through with a new ukulele.

Dear Ann Landers: I'm twenty-four, been married less than a year, and I'm ready to give my bride back to her father. Things I once considered cute now get on my nerves. When she used to get mad and pout, I thought it was adorable. Now I'd like to paste her one in the mush and put her lower lip back where it belongs. Last night we were watching TV. I sat through two hours of junk because she wanted to watch certain shows. Then I said, "OK, now I want to see Lassie." She said, "That's not a real dog. It's a person in an animal outfit and I don't want to see it." I insisted on getting the channel so she pulled the plug out of the wall and said, "All right, then let's both read." I have never hit a woman in my life but I came close that night. Should I talk to her parents?—*Dutch*

Dear Dutch: No. Talk to a marriage counselor—together. If you two have been married less than a year, you're still in the adjustment period. Maybe you do a few things that irritate her and she retaliates via the boob tube. A professional counselor can provide you with unbiased and useful advice.

Dear Ann Landers: Some teen-age girls complain because their parents don't like the boy with whom they are going steady. My problem is the opposite. My mother likes my boyfriend too much, and I wish she'd cut it out. Whenever Bruce calls on the phone and my mother answers, she hangs on for about twenty minutes. She knows very well he didn't call to talk to her, so why does she do it? My mother is young-looking and has a knockout figure. She loves to dance and is very good. She is always asking Bruce to dance with her, and of course he can't refuse. When they dance I get so annoyed I leave the room. If there is something wrong with my attitude, please tell me and I'll try to do better.—*Maybe Jealous*

Dear Maybe: Girls with young mothers often have the same feelings you expressed in your letter. Tell your mother how you feel instead of boiling inside. Sometimes a mother who didn't enjoy her own girlhood tries to live it again through her daughter. Understanding can help.

Dear Ann Landers: I'm a GI stationed in Vietnam. Back home I was never a hotshot with the girls. Here I can have my pick. These chicks go big for Americans. About four months ago I met a beautiful girl who treats me like a king. I think I want to marry her, but I'm not sure. The girl has a child but was never married. All this probably sounds terrible to you, but over here they look at it differently. In fact, the government helps these girls out and nobody thinks anything of it. All my folks know is that I met a girl and I like her a lot. My father has hinted that I'd better not "do anything rash." Do these marriages work?—*Brink*

Dear Brink: Have you considered how this girl will fit into your home environment? And have you considered how you will look to her out of uniform? Make no commitments. If it's love, it will keep till you get home and can look at this relationship through stateside eyes. After six months, if you still want to marry this girl, that's another matter. If she loves you, she'll be waiting. But make sure your two feet are planted firmly in good old terra firma—and the firma the betta.

Dear Ann Landers: Last night my husband and I gave a cocktail party. Polly, the guest of honor, was never much of a drinker and I was surprised when she became plastered. When Polly complained that it was frightfully hot in the house and began to disrobe, I took her aside and told her she'd had too much to drink. My husband suggested she lie down. She became furious and shouted, "That's a lie. I am just as sober as anyone in this room." Then she fell flat on her face. My husband carried her to a bedroom where she passed out. This morning when we awakened, Polly was gone. A note on the dresser read: "You humiliated me before your guests. I will never forgive you." I am heartsick. Shall I call Polly and try to patch things up? My husband says if he never sees her again it will be too soon.—*Chagrined*

Dear Chag: Polly's note was an attempt to put you on the defensive. Don't fall for it. Make no effort to patch things up. If she apologizes, accept it graciously.

Dear Ann Landers: Right now I am smoking myself to death waiting for my husband to come home. He went to a football game this afternoon with "the boys." It is midnight and he's not back yet. We've been married two years and have no children. We both work, and our marriage is a happy one except for this one bad habit. If he decides to have a few drinks with the fellows after work, he just goes and doesn't bother to call and say he'll be late. When he finally gets home and I ask him why he didn't phone, he says, "I didn't think of it." I'm not the only woman in the world who has this problem. What do other women do?—*Outa My Mind*

Dear Outa: Other women do what *you* do. They worry themselves sick, walk the floor, and ask themselves a thousand times, "Where can he be?" and "Why doesn't he call?" The answers you know very well. He's in some bar, slopped to the eyeballs. And he doesn't call because he's a selfish, inconsiderate heel. But he's *your* heel, and you must live with it as best you can and hope that one day he'll develop some consideration for you.

Dear Ann Landers: Please don't tell me you aren't a lawyer. I know you aren't, but you say you want to help people in trouble and I'm in plenty right now. My wife and I went to an open-air theater last week, and we sat behind a couple of gabby women. My wife asked them twice if they would please be quiet so we could hear the lines. They said they were there to enjoy themselves and if we didn't like it we could find other seats. After twenty minutes of listening to those magpies, my wife lost her temper and slammed the noisier woman over the head with her pocketbook. She let out a blood-curdling scream, and of course everybody craned their necks to see what was going on. The manager rushed over and made a big deal of it. He took our names and asked us to leave. Yesterday my wife received an order to appear in court. The charge is assault and battery. Must we go to court on these trumped-up charges?—*S.L.*

Dear S.L.: Since you already know I am not a lawyer, I don't have to tell you. I will tell you, however, you'd better hire one. What you received was a summons and this means no foolin'.

Dear Ann Landers: The problem: Four children, two adults, one bathroom. The girls, fifteen and seventeen, usually get in first. They spend about twenty minutes (together) putting on makeup and combing each other's hair. This makes the boys, ten and twelve, furious. Some mornings the boys get up early and try to beat their sisters into the bathroom. When they succeed, the girls bang on the door and raise such a ruckus my husband (who doesn't have to go to work until noon) gets out of bed and adds to the bedlam by screaming at them. I've begged my husband for a second bathroom, but he says, "We had nine kids in *our* family and the bathroom was outside. We managed to grow up all right."—*Tired Blood*

Dear Tired: If it's any consolation to you, Madame, a house with four kids and one bathroom is usually happier than a house with four bathrooms and no children. Hold a family conference. Tell the girls what time to go in and what time to get out. Buy them a wall mirror so they can apply their makeup and comb their hair in the bedroom. Make it clear that if the girls don't go in on schedule, they lose their place to the boys. This should end the Battle of the Bathroom, which, incidentally, is an old, familiar all-American sport.

Dear Ann Landers: Jason and I have been married ten years. We have always wanted a family, but for some reason I couldn't get pregnant. After going to a fertility clinic for two years, I finally got the good news. Our baby is due next month. Everything was grand until last week. Jason told me when my time comes to go to the hospital, I should call a taxi and leave the house quietly. He said, "I don't want to know a thing." At first I thought he was kidding, but now I believe he is serious. Last night he said again, "Don't call me until you can say whether it's a boy or a girl." Frankly I am hurt. It seems to me a husband should want to be with his wife at such a time. Is something wrong with him? Should I insist that he come with me or should I go alone?—*Mrs. Count Down*

Dear Mrs.: Of course there's something wrong with him. He's scared. Unless you can get your doctor to put him at ease so that he accompanies you willingly, let him stay home. Panicky husbands faint and get in the way and are more trouble than they are worth.

Dear Ann Landers: In your column the other day you told a woman who is expecting her first child that she should not beg her husband to go to the hospital with her if he does not want to go. You said he would probably faint and get in the way, and it would be better to leave him at home. Please, Ann, don't give advice like that. I am a taxi driver, and no fare gives us drivers heart failure like a woman alone who is on the way to the hospital to have a baby. I've been driving a cab for twenty years. I've had three women like that, and each one took ten years off my life. The first one begged me to let her sit in front. When she got a pain she grabbed hold of my arm—or the steering wheel. We almost hit a pedestrian. I drove the second lady two years later. She sat in back. Every three minutes she beat me on the head with her purse and said, "Can't you go faster?" Finally a squad car spotted me speeding, which was a godsend. They gave us the siren all the way to the hospital, and we made it just in time. I wasn't so lucky with the third lady. She had her baby right in my cab, five blocks from the hospital. I was a nervous wreck for three days. But she named the baby after me, so it wasn't all bad. From now on, Ann, tell your pregnant ladies to call an ambulance if their husbands won't take them to the hospital because ambu-

lances have attendants who are set up for that stuff.—
Mac

Dear Mac: Thanks. I will.

Dear Ann Landers: I nearly dropped my eyeglasses
in the coffee when I read your advice to the forty-
year-old woman who had just learned she was pregnant. You said she should be thrilled yet. Have you
lost your mind? The poor thing told you she has a
married daughter and a son in college. And now she is
going to start in again with diapers, whooping cough
shots, sitters—the whole bit. What's more she is des-
tined to be a lifelong member of PTA. I was forty
when my last child was born. When the fifteenth person told me how happy I should be, I told her to put
that show on the road. It was interesting that no woman with a child under twelve years of age opened
up a mouth—only the dames who had had hysterecto-
mies. I wasn't happy *then* and I'm not happy *now*. The
boy is three years old and driving me around the bend.
Yesterday a woman on the bus asked me what my
grandson's name was and I got so mad I said, "He is
not my grandson, he's my little brother. I am helping
out my mother for the day." So please stop telling forty-year-old women they should be thrilled about having a baby. You haven't had a baby in twenty-eight
years and your memory is short. I am living for the
day I can put this holy terror in school and get off
tranquilizers and back on food.—*A Basket Case*

Dear Case: Your letter sounds as if it were written
at the end of a miserable day. Write to me after you've
had a good night's sleep—in about four years.

Twelve

YOU CAN'T MAKE A SILK PURSE

*God grant me the serenity to accept the
things I cannot change—*

The courage to change the things I can—

And the wisdom to know the difference.

Dear Ann Landers: My wife and I have been married twelve years. She still undresses at night in the clothes closet with the lights turned off. I mentioned this casually because I didn't want to make an issue of it. She became upset and said I was a sex maniac. That was five years ago, and I haven't brought it up since. We have two children and are happily married. I have no other complaints. If you can tell me why my wife behaves this way, I will find it easier to accept.—*Black Out*

Dear Black Out: A woman who must hide from her husband while undressing (for twelve years yet) has some warped ideas which were undoubtedly drummed into her when she was a child. In an effort to teach their children modesty parents sometimes, give the impression that there is something evil about the body. These children grow up ashamed and inhibited. They feel they must hide that which is evil, and darkness is best for hiding.

Dear Ann Landers: I am one of those wives who undresses in the closet. I need your help, Ann, not your criticism. I've been married twenty-one years, and our marriage is not great but it's tolerable. I do not have a warped mind or guilt feelings about my body. I undress in the closet because I need my rest. My husband can fall into bed half dead but if I remove a stocking in his presence he suddenly springs back to life. We have four young children, and I do all my own work. If I can manage to sneak into bed with a hairnet on and my face creamed, I can figure on seven hours of sleep instead of six. Other wives around the country must have this problem, too, so please, Ann, get in our corner! We need you.—*Just Tired*

And then a man got into the act:

Dear Ann Landers: The wife who undresses in the closet and signed herself Just Tired is more than just tired. She is Plenty Stupid. The average American housewife and mother leads a fairly busy life, depending on the size of her family, the quality of her housekeeping, and whether she has help. But when the end of the day finds the woman hiding in the closet for fear her husband may get ideas, it is more than a matter of "needing her rest." It means the wife has a lopsided scale of values and her husband is at the bottom of the scale. Cooks and housekeepers are for hire, but certain wifely activities should not be delegated. Some women learn this too late. Others, not at all.—*Old Codger*

Dear Codger: You have a point. Here's an assist from a female who wishes she had the problem:

Dear Ann Landers: Certain wives are luckier than others. For example, the wife whose husband is so amorous she must undress in the closet. What I wouldn't

give to see a gleam in my husband's eye, day *or* night. For years I've been trying to pump some life into our marriage but my husband is always "tired," or should I be honest and say he is not interested?
—*Batting Zero*

Dear Ann Landers: Of all the silly squabbles in your column the one about the wife who undresses in the closet takes the cake. So far as I could tell the woman didn't say she *slept* in the closet, did she? All she did was undress there. It was unfair of you to suggest that she was peculiar. Do you feel, Ann Landers, that it is a wife's duty to put on a nightly striptease for her husband? Do you honestly believe a man would not think about sex unless he was treated to some visual stimulation? Any male who is *that* dead sexually would not bat an eye at the sight of a woman disrobing. A man who is interested in romance will let a woman know. If he is tired and not interested, he deserves to be left alone. To deliberately arouse a husband who has fallen into bed exhausted after a hard day's work is inconsiderate, and it could cause him to feel inadequate. Speaking for myself, I wouldn't dream of undressing in the closet. I undress in the bathroom.—*From Georgia*

Dear Ann Landers: If some of those closet-hiders could stay in there all day as well as at bedtime, they could avoid cooking, shopping, cleaning, and laundry —everything! Why be only half a wife? With a little ingenuity a woman could get out of the whole business.—*Jed*

Dear Jed: The next letter sounds like a buddy of yours. I sense collusion.

Dear Ann: If that dizzy dame has been undressing in the closet for twelve years, it's no wonder her husband "suddenly springs to life" when he sees her remove a stocking. I'll bet by this time the poor guy lights up like a Polish Church when she takes off her hat.—*Sympathetic*

I was happy to close the closet door. I am accustomed to finding skeletons in closets, not wives.

Dear Ann Landers: Thanks for nothing. So you have been picking up after your husband for twenty-nine years and you want another twenty-nine, do you? Well, lots of luck. My husband came home last night, dropped his coat and hat on the floor, and said, "Ann Landers says you should pick it up." I told him his clothes would go out of style before I picked them up. I've got six kids to run after, three meals to fix, lunch boxes to pack, a nine-room house, and laundry stacked to the ceiling. I fall in bed exhausted every night, and *you* think I should play nursemaid to a 220-pound slob with a warped sense of humor. A friend of mine told me she heard you are a man. I'm sure she is right. No woman would write such crazy advice.—*Former Reader*

Dear Former: By the time a man marries he is either an established dropper or a confirmed picker-upper. If you married a dropper, resign yourself. Don't let his bad habits turn you into a nag. If you married a picker-upper, send your mother-in-law a dozen roses.

Dear Ann Landers: I wouldn't have believed it could happen to me a third time, but it has. My youngest daughter eloped with a fellow she met two months ago at the beach. This gives me a perfect record. I am now the mother-in-law of three bums. All my girls are beautiful and have lovely figures. They are intelligent, hold fine jobs, and could have made good marriages.

But no, they go for men who can't make a living and kick them around besides. My oldest daughter has left her husband three times since March. She is never without a black eye or a bruise. The middle girl came home with her suitcase and a broken collarbone. Her husband drinks and goes off his rocker every Friday night. And now my youngest daughter married a loafer who would rather collect unemployment compensation than work. Please explain why girls deliberately choose abusive and unworthy men?—*H.S.M.*

Dear H.S.M.: Some girls think they can turn that sow's ear into a silk purse. They don't realize that after the bloom is off the romance, any attempt at reform is considered nagging. Psychiatrists tell us that women who put up with repeated physical abuse are sick. They feel worthless and inferior, and unconsciously they seek out men who will punish them.

Dear Ann Landers: I've been reading your column for years and have never seen a problem like mine. My son's mother-in-law telephones me at least twice a week to complain about something my son did or did not do. For instance, this morning Mrs. Pain-in-the-Neck called me at 7:30 A.M. and said, "Your son left for High Point this morning and didn't leave Marcella any money. He won't be back until tomorrow and the poor girl hasn't got a dime. I'll have to take some money over to her right away." Last week she called to tell me my son gave Marcella only one hour's notice and brought three business friends home for cocktails. Marcella didn't have any soda or lemons in the house. The place was a mess, and she didn't even have time to comb her hair. Marcella happens to be a lazy, disorganized slob. I don't want to become involved in their troubles, and I don't want Mrs. Pain-in-the-Neck to tell me what goes on between them. What do you recommend?—*H.J.K.*

Dear H.J.K.: The next time Mrs. Pain-in-the-Neck calls say this: "It breaks my heart that a fine, lovely girl like Marcella married a worthless, no-good bum like my son. She could have done much better, and I'm sorry she didn't. Please don't tell me any more sad stories about those two because it spoils my whole day."

Dear Ann Landers: We've been married twenty years and have two children ten and eight years of age. I've worked like a horse for the last fifteen years and I'm tired. We own a small café which I run myself. My husband has a little business on the other side of town which requires his attention three days a week. I do all my own cooking, housework, washing and ironing, and the yard work. I put in a good fifteen-hour day. When I mention quitting work my husband's blood pressure zooms, and he yells, "Fine idea—why don't we *both* quit and starve to death?" He likes the café business because it gives him a chance to sit around and chin with the customers. He fancies himself a poor man's Toots Shor. Is it a crime to want to stay home and take care of my children? How do I get out of this rut? —*Disgusted*

Dear Disgusted: From your description of the ball o' fire you're married to, you just might starve if you quit running the café. So here's a suggestion which is practical and fair: Split the café work with the genial host. Make it clear you are taking off two full days a week. On the days he sits around "chinning with the customers" tell him to take over for a few hours while you go home. Then *go.*

Dear Ann Landers: I just read the letter from Invisible Wife who complained because her husband never noticed anything about her. She redid her hair, lost forty pounds, and even had her teeth fixed. Everyone raved about the "New Her," but her ever-lovin' spouse never said one word. I'd like to trade husbands with that woman. My boob doesn't miss a detail. If there is a speck of dust under the bed or a wrinkle in a shirt, he'll find it. If my nail polish is chipped or if I have a crooked hem or a run in my stocking, he calls it to my attention. Naturally if I mispronounce a word, he corrects me in front of everybody. So, Ann Landers, tell the lady with the Silent Man to stop complaining. She's better off than she thinks.—*Permanent Target*

Dear Ann Landers: We've been married fourteen years and my husband still carries his shirts over to his mother's house because I don't iron them to suit him. I iron organdy curtains well enough so that everyone who comes into the house asks me if they are new. My daughter won first prize in the school Halloween costume contest. She was a rosebud. I ironed two thousand petals before I sewed them on her dress. Do you think I ought to insist that my husband leave his shirts for me to do—as a matter of pride?—*Pearlie*

Dear Pearlie: So long as your husband's mother is alive and able to iron his shirts she's going to do it. Accept the situation and consider it your good fortune. Millions of women would be happy if they could get someone to help them with their ironing—for free yet.

Dear Ann Landers: We've been married three years and my wife is a mess. She won't tell me how much weight she has gained, but she must weigh over two hundred pounds. I could tolerate her size if she weren't so lazy. She has every known appliance to make her housework easier, but she's too "tired" to plug in anything. She has never used her sewing machine even though her clothes are all torn at the seams. She irons nothing, not even a handkerchief. Cooking is out of the question. Her hobby is talking on the telephone and eating candy. Our two-year-old child doesn't get enough fresh air or sunshine because her mother is too busy to take her outside. My wife has gone to three doctors, and nobody has been able to help her lose weight. Please suggest something.—Had It

Dear Had It: Usually letters which begin like yours wind up with, "and now I have met a lovely woman." It's a familiar story. When a wife refuses to shape up, the husband often ships out. Your wife is more than lazy, she's sick in the head. A woman who refuses to accept her responsibilities and eats like a pig needs psychiatric help.

Dear Ann Landers: Three of my closest friends are divorcees with children. For years I've been hearing about their problems. The solutions always seemed obvious and easy to me, since I was not emotionally involved. Six months ago I divorced my husband after fifteen years of marriage. I have discovered to my amazement that those "easy solutions" aren't so easy. Can you explain why a man who has ignored his children throughout their lives suddenly gets attacks of paternal devotion after a divorce? What compels him to take his sons to baseball and football games, and fishing? I used to beg him to take them for an ice-cream cone, but he was always too busy. Why does the divorced father buy his daughters expensive and impractical gifts and telephone them "just to talk"? When he was living in the house he never bought them a thing, and he couldn't think of a word to say. Why the change? Can you tell me in a word?—*Mystified*

Dear Mystified: Yes. Guilt.

Dear Ann Landers: My husband and I have been married for forty long, boring, miserable, rotten years. I don't know how a woman of my intelligence and refinement could have chosen such a coarse, vulgar man. All these years we have existed under the same roof, although we have nothing in common. He loves dirty jokes, hunting and fishing, and plenty of sex. I am soft-spoken, cultured, and genteel. Next year the slob retires, and the thought of having him at home under my feet all day gives me a sick feeling at the pit of my stomach. I want to do some traveling with people of my own class. We are financially able to take some lovely trips, but he'd rather hunt and fish with his low-brow friends. I am still attractive and could enjoy the companionship of a high-type man. Would a divorce at age sixty-two be such a terrible thing?—*A Real Lady*

Dear Lady: Your letter shows no trace of gentility, refinement, or culture. And soft-spoken you aren't, kiddo. If your husband has been able to stand *you* for almost half a century, you'd better not press your luck. Stay where you are and travel when he goes hunting and fishing.

Dear Ann Landers: My wife is one of the sweetest girls in the world. Delores has given me a fine family, and we have everything we could ask for. The problem is her drinking, but she's not a lush. After one cocktail Delores gets into arguments and says insulting things to her best friends. When she remembers what she said the next day, she goes into a depression. After two drinks she passes out, cold as a mackerel. She never drinks at home—only when we go out. This has been going on for two years. Every time it happens, Delores takes an oath on her mother's life that she will never touch another drop of alcohol, but when she gets out of my sight at a party, she's as good as passed out. What can I do to help her?—*D.F.L.*

Dear D.F.L.: Your wife's form of alcoholism is unusual. She needs help. It's useless, however, to try to force help on people who do not believe they need it. When (and if) she expresses the need for help, suggest A.A.

Dear Ann Landers: I am getting sick and tired of reading that same old worn-out phrase in your column: "When you marry a divorced man you marry the whole package—the ex-mate, the kids, the ex-in-laws, old friends, and so on." You gotta be crazy. I married a divorced man and there's nothing in my marriage contract that says I have to be bothered with any of the aforementioned kooks. My husband's ex-wife is a religious fanatic who reads the Bible with one hand and drinks gin with the other. Her children are going to be just like her. American courts seem to have the insane idea that children are better off with their mother, even if she is a nut, so I say let her paddle her own canoe. And why don't you talk about something else for a change?—*Outspoken*

Dear Out: It's easy to say, "Let her paddle her own canoe," but that canoe has your husband's kids in it. If this woman is as nutty as you say, and if your husband is halfway decent, he will keep in close touch with his children. This means you are going to be "in touch," too, Madame—whether you like it or not.

Dear Ann Landers: My boyfriend is a high-school senior. Butch is not the greatest student in the world but he's a terrific athlete and has a wonderful personality. My girl friends make fun of Butch because they say he talks like he was born in a foreign country.

He was born right here in Buffalo. His parents were born in Europe, and they speak their native language at home. Butch pronounces certain words wrong, but then nobody is perfect. He says "Babe Root" instead of "Babe Ruth," "dem" for "them," and "wacation" instead of "vacation." When he said "Walley Forge" in class everyone broke up. Should I correct Butch when he makes mistakes or would it be best to say nothing and hope that he catches on by himself?—*Butch's Girl*

Dear Girl: A high-school boy who says "Babe Root" and "Walley Forge" is not likely to catch on by himself. Speak to Butch privately about the words he mispronounces. He picked up these speech habits from his parents, and it's going to take a lot of work to unlearn them.

Dear Ann Landers: Our handsome twenty-two-year-old son has had several crushes. The girl he is going with now is short and dumpy. She has a homely, expressionless face. Her taste in clothes is atrocious. A soiled brassiere strap is always hanging out. The girl is so ignorant I don't know how she got out of high school. The note she wrote thanking me for her birthday cake had eleven mistakes. Our son has brought her home for dinner five times. I wonder if we are being too hospitable. I don't want our son to interpret our kindness to this girl as approval. On the other hand I'm afraid to be unfriendly because he might end up marrying her. Please advise.—*Thinking Ahead*

Dear Thinking: I applaud you for being hospitable, although it's obvious you dislike the girl intensely. In my view you have chosen the wise approach.

Dear Ann Landers: My wife is Pennsylvania Dutch. They are supposed to be the cleanest people on the face of the earth, and my wife is determined to prove it. In the meantime the kids and I are like in jail. Our carpets have never been walked on. She has knitted booties for everybody. Each person who comes into our home has to park his shoes by the door. Nobody has ever seen our lovely furniture because my wife has draped sheets over everything. If you offered me ten dollars right now to tell you the color of our sofa, I couldn't do it. Please print my letter so the guys with sloppy wives will realize that maybe they haven't got it so bad after all.—*Germ-Free*

Dear Germ: Your wife is more than neat. She has a geranium in her cranium. My condolences to you and the children.

Dear Ann Landers: Recently you printed a letter from a young bride whose groom cried on his wedding night because he was lonesome for his mother. Anyone who thinks that letter was a fake because such a thing just couldn't happen is lucky. I know how real it is because I married a man who had the identical problem. When the minister finished the ceremony (this was thirty-two years ago) he said, "You may now kiss the bride." My groom turned to me and said, "Later, dear, I can't kiss you in front of my mother." I was so upset I told him to get professional help or I would have the marriage annulled. He had several sessions with a psychiatric social worker which helped a lot. The real change came when our minister pointed out that the Bible says a man should put his wife before his mother. He had never heard of this before. I don't know if this letter makes sense to women who don't have the problem, but maybe it's worth printing for the benefit of young girls who are going with mamma's boys.—*Muskegon*

Dear Ann Landers: My wife took a few lessons in voice before we were married eighteen years ago. The truth is she can't carry a note with a cosinger. Whenever we go to a party, Isobel gets a few beers and wants to give a recital. What Isobel does best is the hog-calling bit. She was raised near Ida Grove, Iowa, and won the county hog-calling championship for three straight years. When the party gets going good, everyone hollers, "Call the hogs, Isobel," but she wants to sing opera; they want her specialty. Isobel says it isn't dignified. Please tell her to be a sport. She thinks you're great and she'll listen to you.—*Buck*

Dear Buck: Since I'm an Iowa girl myself I can tell you that a good hog-caller has something to be proud of. That "Soo—eeeey—sooey-sooey" bit is an art. C'mon, Isobel, give the folks what they want.

Dear Ann Landers: Why would any husband adore a lazy, messy, disorganized, addlebrained wife? Her house looks like they moved in yesterday. For two years she has been saying, "We're not settled yet." To top it off, he is a handsome guy and she is nothing to look at. She never cooks a meal. Everything is in cans or frozen. Her kids eat so much sent-in Chinese food I wouldn't be surprised if their eyes began to slant. Yet this slob's husband treats her like a Dresden doll. He calls her Poopsie and Pet and covers the telephone with a blanket when he goes to work so she can get her rest. On weekends he does the laundry and the marketing. I get up at 6 A.M. and fix my husband a farmer's breakfast. I make his shirts because the ones in the stores "don't fit right." If my husband ever emptied a wastebasket I'd faint. Once I phoned him at work and asked him to drop by the store on his way home and pick up a loaf of bread. He swore at me for five minutes. The more you do for a man the less he appreciates you. I feel like a housekeeper not a wife. What goes on anyway?—*The Moose* (That's what he calls *me*.)

Dear Moose: A man doesn't love a woman because she keeps the house spotless and shines his shoes. He can hire those services. You can call the wife next door addlebrained if you want to—and maybe she is —but when it comes to handling her husband she's a genius. The woman who knows how to make her husband feel that he is her hero has it made.

Dear Ann Landers: Recently I read your advice to the wife who said she felt like an "unpaid housekeeper." The woman described her spotless home, beautiful meals—and she even shined her husband's shoes. Yet he showed no appreciation whatever. You said, "The woman who knows how to make her husband feel that he is her hero has it made." I would give anything in the world if I could do just that. How does a woman make her husband feel like "her hero"? —*Also Unappreciated*

Dear Also: How did you treat the fellows you dated when you wanted to make a wonderful impression? Test your memory, kiddo, and replay the tape. You laughed at his jokes, built him up, and made him feel special and important. You treated him with courtesy and respect. You waited until you were alone if you had some criticism you just *had* to get out. A successful marriage is not a gift; it is an achievement. The effort and energy that a woman puts into her marriage is like money in the bank. It begets interest in the form of strength, confidence, and stability. When the going gets rough you have something to draw from. A marriage license is not a guarantee that the marriage is going to work, any more than a fishing license assures you that you'll catch fish. It merely gives you the legal right to try.

Thirteen

TEEN-AGE SEX—PUT OUT OR HOLD OUT?

Dear Teen-Ager: You've written me over a million letters. It's time I wrote you one. I'm not as pessimistic about your generation as some people. I don't happen to buy the idea that most of your leisure time is spent sniffing glue, smoking marihuana, tripping out on LSD, killing yourselves on the highways, and having sex orgies five nights a week. Ninety-seven percent of you kids have never been arrested and probably never will be.

You are, on the whole, more sensitive than your parents, less prejudiced, and less willing to settle for shoddy values. I know, too, that in some ways your life is easier than theirs was when they were teen-agers, and I wish they would stop telling you about it. In many ways your life is more difficult. They had money problems. You have identity problems.

I've come to know you well through your letters, and I have met thousands of you face-to-face. You've been courteous and responsive when I lectured in your schools from Buffalo to Los Angeles, from Minneapolis to Miami. And not just white Anglo-Saxon Protestant Showcase schools. The all-Negro high school in Greenville, Mississippi (this was 1965), was no showcase, but the students were marvelous. They reaffirmed my faith in the potential of all people who have an opportunity to live decently and get a good education.

A great many adults are concerned about your morals. They say you are sleeping around a lot and they worry about it. There is some justification for their concern.

In the past twenty years the number of unwed mothers has tripled. Venereal disease is at an all-time high, in spite of penicillin. In some areas, V.D. has reached epidemic proportions. Forty percent of all teen-age brides are pregnant when they get married.

Some authorities in the field of sex education believe it is ridiculous to condemn premarital sex. "What's the use?" they cry. "When we tell kids to save sex for marriage they look at us like we had holes in our heads. The best we can hope for is to teach them sexual responsibility."

One prominent leader in Planned Parenthood said, "Premarital sex should be entered into as a faithful episode. Choose your mate carefully, and so long as you go with that particular party, don't sleep with anyone else." He adds this last-minute bit of advice, "Remember to use effective controls."

What he means, of course, is, "If you can't be good, be careful."

An attractive middle-aged housewife made it abundantly clear on a TV network program recently that The Pill was a "Godsend." "Since the pill," she said, "I am a new woman. I give it to my teen-age daughter and I sleep much better now."

Such reasoning represents total capitulation and unspoken condonation. It is the same as leaving this note for a burglar: "Dear Friend: I know you are here to crack the safe. It won't be necessary. Here is the combination. Please take what you want and don't destroy anything."

My position on premarital sex is plain and simple. Premarital sex is dumb. It is dumb because it violates

the moral and ethical rules of our society. And don'
say, "The rules are wrong." Maybe some of them are,
but they are the rules, and rules should be obeyed.
When we disregard rules we pay a penalty, and the
penalty for premarital sex is usually guilt, self-depreca-
tion, worry, and a sullied reputation. Sometimes the
penalty is V.D. or pregnancy.

The girl who gives herself to her steady "to prove
her love" often becomes disenchanted when the Romance of the Century turns out to be something less
than perfect. She considers herself "damaged goods."
A girl who has lost her virginity tends to become
promiscuous because she feels she has nothing to lose.

And then there's fear. Fear of pregnancy, fear of
disease, fear of getting found out, fear of being
dumped. And when he dumps you, there's the fear of
being abandoned. He was the most important thing in
your life. What now? The whole ugly scene is a nightmare I have heard described a thousand times. "It's
too late for me," they write, "but please warn the girls
who haven't yet made the foolish mistake. Tell them
it's not worth it."

Sex is not a plaything. It is God's plan for perpet-
uating life. And it is something more. It is the perfect
way to express complete love and devotion. This kind
of emotional investment requires judgment and maturity.

Boys and girls operate on different wavelengths. She
has the romantic image of love as it is portrayed in the
movies. She envisions the boy as her knight in shining
armor. He will protect her, stand by her, cherish her.
Sexual intercourse will bind them together forever.
This is love.

The boy is thinking, too—but not about love. Most
boys are thinking about making out. Boys make out
for a variety of reasons, most usually because it is eas-

er to find a girl who will say Yes than to control their physical urges. It is a glandular response rather than a spiritual commitment. Many boys make out to prove their manhood. And some boys make out because they want to brag to their peers.

Whether you are going to be a Hold-Out or a Put-Out is *your* decision. No matter how strict your parents are they cannot police you twenty-four hours a day. If you want to slip your collar, you'll find a way. I urge you to make the decision on the basis of whether or not it will be beneficial for you. Weigh the arguments for and against. What do you stand to gain? What do you stand to lose? Will sexual relations add to your inner security and peace of mind? Will it enhance your feeling of personal worth? If you should become pregnant, what would it do to your life—to your family? And if you believe The Pill is the answer, forget it. It isn't, for high-school girls. The Pill must be taken under a doctor's supervision to be a hundred percent effective.

Think it over. It could be the most important decision of your life.

Dear Ann Landers: I am a high-school girl who believes in free love. There are plenty more like me. I am not a pushover. I come from a high-class family and I make good grades. I see nothing wrong with sleeping with different boys so long as I like them and they like me—as a person, I mean. Virginity is an old-fashioned idea that makes no sense anymore. Why should a girl save herself for a man who is not making any great effort to save himself for her? In our social group I don't know of a single guy who has done much of a preservation job. Sex is an important part of marriage, and I want to be the perfect wife. The practice I am getting now will be very useful when Mr. Right comes along. So you see, there *are* logical and sensible arguments against virginity.—*Miss Honest*

Dear Miss: If you are sleeping around to get experience for Mr. Right, you can stop now. Mr. Right will not view your list of bed-partners as impressive credentials. In fact, he might get the idea that you are a tramp. I don't expect to cut any mustard with you, Toots, but for the girls who have not yet lost the Great Debate, I'd like to say this: Insofar as sex is concerned, practice *does not* make perfect. It *does* make juicy conversation in locker rooms, and of course it can also make babies, as the young girl who wrote the next letter discovered.

Dear Ann Landers: I just read the letter from "Miss Honest," the high school girl who believes in free love and sees nothing wrong with going to bed with a boy if she "likes him as a person." The letter could have been written by me five years ago. I put up the same foolish arguments. Here is how my life turned out, and I am only twenty-two. I was married at seventeen—three months' pregnant. Bill and I have been married three years and separated five times. I started divorce proceedings six months ago and discovered I was pregnant again, so we called off the divorce and are trying to work things out. I am so tired of sex I could scream. It used to be all I lived for and now I despise it. I talked to my doctor, and he told me that due to my early promiscuity I have become disoriented sexually and I need psychiatric help. I had to go look up some words in the dictionary, and what it boils down to is this: I ran around so much when I was in my early teens that sex lost its value and now I hate it. I hope Miss Free Love, and all the other young girls who think they can play this game and get away with it, will learn something from my experience. Believe me, Ann, I am—*Paying Dearly.*

Dear Paying: I hope you will take your doctor's advice. The first step is understanding the problem, and you do, so get going.

Dear Ann Landers: I am a sixteen-year-old and I attend a large high school in New York. The kids in school talk a lot about sex, and I can tell you that most of them do more than just talk. My best friend has been sleeping with her boyfriend, but I am not writing to criticize her. What I need is some answers. We have had lots of arguments about right and wrong, and I have been losing. My friend says she is in love, and sex is the natural way to express complete devotion. She also says if she refused to go along, her boyfriend would drop her and find someone more cooperative. When I asked what she would do if she got pregnant, she laughed and said, "The Pill never fails." Please tell me how to win these arguments.—*Out-Talked*

Dear Out: Why bother? Your girl friend has already lost the most important argument. Now she is trying to justify her position. I have had letters from other teen-age girls who also laughed and said, "The Pill never fails." They stopped laughing when the doctor said, "You're pregnant." Assuming that pregnancy can be avoided, it is still foolish for high-school kids to play house. Why? Because our society has decreed that sex belongs in marriage. Sex on the sneak can be ugly, frightening, and disappointing. It can create guilt, resentment, and a totally unrealistic concept of what life and love are all about. If it's love, it can wait. If it isn't, who needs it?

Dear Ann Landers: I am nineteen and going with a very smart fellow who is majoring in psychology. He is twenty. He tells me I am unrealistic, antediluvian, selfish, stubborn and mid-Victorian. Why? Because I don't believe that the physical pleasures of marriage should be enjoyed by couples who are going steady. According to my boyfriend, a girl should prepare for marriage if she wants to be a successful wife in the same way that a pianist should have hours of rehearsal before he enters Carnegie Hall to play a concert. He says if a girl has had no premarital experience, marriage can be a shock. Like I said, he is very smart.—*Sinking*

Dear Sinking: Tell that smart boyfriend of yours that pregnancy outside of marriage can be a bigger shock than marriage without experience.

Dear Ann Landers: I had to smile when I read the letter from the girl who was advocating free love. She wrote as if she had invented something. I'll bet many people have the idea that free love is part of the "new morality"—something modern. I am fifty-three years old and heard the same guff forty years ago. My older sister was a teen-ager at the end of World War I. Free love was very big among the nonconformist thinkers. When I talked to my mother about it (she is seventy-six now), she told me there were free-love champions in *her* day. "Of course they were sneakier about it," she laughed, "but we all knew who they were." Interesting how the abused and degraded institution of marriage survives through the ages in spite of the people who ignore it and insist they have found something better. It's enough to make a girl decide that maybe it's smart to be "old-fashioned."—*Observer Of The Passing Scene*

Dear Ann Landers: I am the father of three preteen daughters, and I read your column every day. Frankly, I am worried to death about the permissive So-What-Why-Not attitude toward sex among today's teen-agers. Recently, a sixteen-year-old girl wrote in to ask you why she shouldn't sleep with her boyfriend. She said he was becoming increasingly insistent and she was afraid if she didn't give in soon he would drop her in favor of someone who was more cooperative. Have we parents failed so miserably in our attempts to instill decent values in our daughters that they would prostitute themselves in order to hang onto a boyfriend who isn't worth a hill of beans in the first place? Surely, *all* teen-agers don't feel this way. I would like to see some letters in your column from girls who consider themselves real people rather than playthings and sex objects. Do such teens actually exist?—*Father of Girls*

Dear Ann Landers: I would like to respond to the father of three daughters. He wanted to know if there are any decent girls left? The answer is Yes. And it's not because I haven't had a chance to be otherwise. I have been out with every type of male—from the mamma's boy who wouldn't dream of touching a girl to the sex maniac who views every date as a challenge to fight the lady to the floorboard. I decided when I started to date that any girl who would trade her virginity for a dinner and a movie has to be a nitwit. And any boy who would suggest such a trade (no matter how subtly) is a foolish, egotistical jackass and should be treated like one.—*Intact in Illinois*

Dear Ann Landers: I am a high-school senior who decided at age twelve that I would never buy a cheap package of kicks. I've heard plenty of sales pitches. Some were smoother than others, but they all added up to the same thing—a shoddy proposition. I'm sure it was my parents, especially my father (an obstetrician), who gave me and my sisters our basic ideas about sex. I'll always be grateful they never made us feel sex was dirty or wrong. When Dad would tell us about an unwed mother who had been in his office, he did so with compassion, not disgust. He pointed out that most of the unwed mothers who were brought to him by welfare agencies were ignorant little girls, some of them fourteen and fifteen years old. These girls were lonely and they felt unloved. They mistakenly believed that an invitation to sex meant someone cared about them and wanted them. He also pointed out that the boys who got these girls into trouble were usually ignorant and irresponsible kids or married men who were looking for anything from anybody. To my way of thinking, holding out has never meant the difference between being a good girl or a bad girl. It has meant the choice between being sensible and disciplined or foolish and weak. While I am pleased with my choice, it is my parents who deserve the credit.—*One Of Many*

Dear Ann Landers: Count me as one who considers herself a real person and not a plaything or a sex object. It is not easy to hold out in this world of rapidly changing values. The standard concepts of morality are not as universally accepted as they once were. Two often they fall flat when challenged by space-age arguments for sexual involvement. Lofty ideals are fine, but a girl needs something more tangible these days. Here are the thoughts that have kept me straight for nineteen years: One day I hope to meet a man who will love me, admire me, and respect me. I want to be worthy of him. Maybe he'll be a free thinker and won't care if I am a virgin or not. But maybe he'll be an old-fashioned guy and he'll care a lot. No man would mind marrying a virgin, but there are plenty of men to whom it might make a great deal of difference. I'm not taking any chances.—*Hands Off*.   e

Letters like these make me feel pretty good about the human race, and then I get one like this next beaut:

Dear Ann Landers: Our twenty-year-old son returned home from college for Easter vacation. He said, "Mom and Dad, I hope you will be objective about this. I've got a date tonight. The girl is a sure thing. I know I can score. May I use my bedroom or are you going to force me to use the car?" We have two sons, Ann. The other boy is nineteen, and we are permitting them both to use their bedrooms. I feel we are being realistic and modern. Our friends are horrified. We know you are a moralist but we also know you are a realist. Express yourself, Madame.—*Winnetka Parents*

Dear Winnetka: The fact that your sons would ask for permission to bring girls to their bedrooms tells me what they think of your morals. Your approval of this wild request is evidence that they did not misjudge you. If one of your "modern" sons gets a not-so-modern girl pregnant, will you be able to look her parents in the eye and accept your share of the responsibility?

The following letter may well have been written by one of the girls who went to Winnetka.

Dear Ann Landers: You keep getting letters from "Hold-Outs" who are depressed because they have no dates. They say the "Put-Outs" seem to be having a ball, and they wonder if the boys who ask, "What are you saving it for?" don't have a point. Ann, I'm a "Put-Out," and I'd gladly change places with the "Hold-Out." I get asked out every night of the week, and I'm sick of creeps who head straight for the park. I am also sick of myself. Nine guys out of ten can't be trusted to keep their mouths shut. Whenever I meet a new fellow I wonder how much he has heard about me, and usually he has heard plenty. I'm seventeen and my reputation isn't worth a plugged nickel. Please pass the word.—*Ashamed Of My Popularity*

Dear Ashamed: Consider it passed.

Dear Ann Landers: You are a menace to society. You really gave every irresponsible skirt-chasing male in the world the green light when you said on a TV program recently, "Unless a boy uses chloroform or a lead pipe, the girl is responsible for whatever happens to her." For twenty years I have been a housemother for unmarried mothers. These girls are victims of weapons far more deadly than chloroform or lead pipes. They are sweet words of love and empty promises. It's high time parents taught their sons that girls are not playthings to be used for pleasure and then cast aside if something goes wrong. Every young man should be taught that a decent boy is responsible for his girl. Several of my pregnant girls saw and heard you make that remark, and they became depressed because you placed all the blame on them. This letter is to let you know that I am canceling the subscription to the paper that prints your column.—*Housemother*

Dear Housemother: You are right when you say a decent boy should be responsible for his girl, but not all boys are decent. Moreover, out-of-wedlock pregnancies involve more than decency. There are such factors as permissive parents, sexy movies, liquor, unchaperoned parties, midnight beach blasts, and going steady. Most sixteen-year-old boys are not thinking about love and marriage. The juices are flowing and the boys are out looking for kicks. The girl is responsible for whatever happens to her because some boys will take whatever they can get plus whatever they can talk a girl in to. She'd better know it and conduct herself accordingly.

Dear Ann Landers: Are you on vacation or what? Who gave that rotten advice blaming the parents of young boys who get into trouble? And that idiotic phrase from a reader about "robbing a young girl of her maidenhood"—he's got to be kidding. In most cases it could scarcely be called a robbery. During the eleven years I've been a juvenile court officer I've seen hundreds of pregnant girls under sixteen. Most of them have been with so many boys that they can't remember their names. When they get into trouble they point a finger at some yokel who had too much to drink, and the court takes their word against his. And what about the tramps who get pregnant intentionally—so they can wring a nice settlement out of a guy with rich parents or a married man who can't afford the publicity? Why don't *you* wake up and smell the coffee?—*Seen It All*

When I told "Seen It" that having a baby out of wedlock is a hard way to make money, I was bombarded with letters from the mothers of boys who had gotten girls in trouble. Most of them sounded like this one:

Dear Ann Landers: You have done more damage to the image of the unwed father than anyone in North America. Our son is a fine young man nineteen years of age. Every time you print a letter from an unwed mother he shows it to me and says, "Why doesn't Ann Landers ever say anything good about *us?* We have a side, too." Are you so blind that you don't realize some girls run after boys, ply them with liquor, and

offer themselves in such a way that no male could refuse? This is what happened to our son. Yet he was called terrible names and ended up with a black eye.
—*Mother Of A Good Son*

Dear Mother: I have yet to hear from an unwed mother who wouldn't rather have a black eye than what she was left with. Sorry, Mom, I don't have any good-conduct medals lying around for unwed fathers. And I don't have any advice for them either. They don't need it. The boy usually goes about his business, free as a bird. Nothing changes for him. And unwed fathers don't write to Ann Landers very often. They don't need my list of maternity homes.

Dear Ann Landers: According to you, the boy who gets a girl in trouble walks off free as a bird while she is left to face the rap, usually alone and disgraced. It's not always that pat. I got a girl pregnant but didn't marry her because it would have been a disaster for us both. She knew it as well as I. We were worlds apart —intellectually, socially, and financially. But to this day (four years have passed) my conscience bothers me and I often think about her and that little boy who was put up for adoption. It's not easy to go from day to day knowing that somewhere you have a child you'll never see. Believe me, I didn't get off easy, Ann. The price was high.—*Still Paying*

Dear Still: Since you and the girl were "worlds apart intellectually, socially, and financially," it's too bad you didn't stay worlds apart physically. Of course you didn't get off easy. Why should you?"

Dear Ann Landers: Recently an irate mother wrote and asked why you never had any kind words for the unwed father. Your reply was very unsympathetic. You said you had no good-conduct medals lying around for unwed fathers and that it was always the girl who paid. You added, "The boy can go about his business. . . . Nothing changes for him." I disagree. I am not an unwed father but my best buddy is. Believe me, he has paid plenty. He got the news when he was a junior in college. He actually wanted to marry the girl but her folks were against it, and she listened to them—not to him. His life changed that very day. He began to feel depressed and couldn't study. His grades went to the dogs. He flunked out and had to take a laborer's job. He is paying child support, and he will continue to pay until the child is twenty-one. The worst of it is the guy feels so guilty and worthless now that he refuses to take out a girl. He doesn't think he's good enough for anybody. Some unwed fathers may be bums, but some are good guys who made a mistake. In this case the girl made a better adjustment than the boy. She recently married a nice fellow and seems to be very happy.—*For Justice*

Dear Justice: You are right. I should not have made such a sweeping generalization. Dozens of parents, social workers and—yes—even unwed mothers, wrote to protest. Each individual deserves to be judged on his own merits, and I am grateful to you and to other readers who reminded me.

Dear Ann Landers: The teen-agers here in Memphis think you are tuned in to our world like no other adult. You must get a ton of mail from teen-agers or you must talk to a lot of kids because you really have the word. Just to keep you posted I am sending a copy of a questionnaire that has been floating around our high school. Nobody knows for sure where this thing got started, but the kids in my crowd, both guys and chicks, think it's pretty good. I would like your opinion of this questionnaire, and I know you will level. Please don't suggest I take it home and get my mother's views. If she saw it she would faint, and we'd have to call the doctor:

KNOW THYSELF QUESTIONNAIRE

(Rate yourself from 1 to 10 for each "Yes" answer.)

1. Ever gone out with a member of the opposite sex? 4
2. Ever been kissed? 4
3. Ever been French-kissed? 4
4. Ever been kissed while in a reclining position? 5
5. Ever gotten or given a hickey? 3
6. Ever been kissed in your pajamas? 2
7. Ever been kissed against your will? 2
8. Ever parked for more than an hour? 5
9. Ever said, "I love you"? 3
10. Ever said, "I love you," to more than one person? 3
11. Ever gone steady? 4
12. Ever been picked up by a person you never saw before? 7
13. Ever played strip poker with a member of the opposite sex? 5
14. Have you gone all the way? 10
15. Have you had the desire to go all the way but managed to keep from it? 2
16. Have you ever made a member of the opposite sex cry? 4
17. Has a member of the opposite sex ever made you you cry? 4
18. Do you smoke? 2
19. Do you drink? 2
20. Ever passed out from drinking? 5
21. Ever lied to your folks about where you went or with whom? 8

22. Ever smoke pot? 7
23. Ever taken an LSD trip? 10
24. Ever considered the pregnancy route so your folks would have to let you get married? 10

Score Chart

9 or under	Queer or something
10 to 15	Pure as the driven snow
15 to 25	Passionate but prudish
25 to 35	Normal and decent
35 to 45	Indecent
45 to 55	Headed for serious trouble
55 to 60	In terrible shape
60 or over	Condemned

Signed—*Normal And Decent*

Dear N And D: I can't evaluate this questionnaire because each questionnaire should be evaluated on the basis of the individual scoring. Let me say it's darned interesting (though somewhat gamy), and I appreciate your sending it.

Dear Ann Landers: I have a girl friend who sent for your booklet called "Necking and Petting and How Far To Go." The booklet arrived in a plain envelope and your name was not on the outside, which was a big relief to her. She read every word of it. Three months later the poor kid had to get married. Everybody was shocked. What I want to know is, why do you send out booklets that don't do any good?—*Vicky*

Dear Vicky: Sorry, dear, my booklets do not carry a guarantee.

Dear Ann Landers: You will swear this letter is a phony because my story reads like a four-bit novel, but

I am begging you to take it seriously because I am on the level. I go to a well-known girls' school in the East. I became engaged to a Princeton senior three months ago. When I went to his home to meet his parents, I flipped over his father. At first I told myself it was too crazy for words and I tried to laugh it off, but I can't laugh anymore, and neither can he. We have met in Manhattan several times, and he is as zonked over me as I am over him. He wants to divorce his wife and marry me next year. My fiancé knows nothing of this. I am tearing myself to pieces with indecision. Could it work? He is twenty-seven years older than I am. His wife is three years older than he is and a semi-invalid. After being with Senior, Junior strikes me as Amateur Knight. Could this marriage possibly work? Help me, please, I am not sleeping very well these nights.—*Miss Icarus* (Get It?)

Dear Miss Icarus: Yeah, I get it, and my advice is to Drop Daedalus—no pun intended. If you can't sleep now, how much sleep do you think you'll get if you allow this aging Romeo to dump his ailing wife and walk off with his son's sweetheart? The man must have rocks in his head, and you have a few sizable boulders yourself, kiddo. This whole scene is a cross between Sigmund Freud and a Greek tragedy. Forget it.

Dear Ann Landers: I am a twenty-two-year-old college student whose world has just crumbled. Last night the twenty-one-year-old girl I'm in love with told me all about herself. I was so ill this morning I couldn't make my 9 A.M. class. Arletta and I have been going together for six months. She is beautiful, gay, and behaves like the model young woman on any campus. Last night she told me that she had given herself to a boy she went steady with in high school. They had talked about marriage, and he persuaded her that she was foolish not to live life to the limit. They went together five months and broke up when he moved to another city. I thought I wanted to marry Arletta but now I'm not sure. If she was able to fool me so completely, will I ever be able to trust her? And how do I know there were not others? Please help me. I'm sick with grief.—*Like Dead*

Dear Like: Better write off Arletta. The way your mind is operating you'll have her pictured as the town's Number One streetwalker within a week. Did she ask you for an affidavit of your purity? If so, would you have been able to produce one? Love is forgiving. It is accepting people as they are. Since you are unable to do this, hunt up a white-flower girl. (And lots of luck, Bub.) I'm not pinning any roses on the guy in the next letter but I think he could teach you something.

Dear Ann Landers: Our oldest son is thirty-three, unmarried, and in the Army. We've been hoping Everett would find a nice girl and settle down. Everett telephoned last night from Texas. He said, "I've met her at last. She's the loveliest girl in the world. We are getting married this weekend." I was thrilled. Then he said, "I think I ought to tell you she is pregnant and that the baby isn't mine. But I want to marry her anyway." I thought I was hearing things, Ann, like maybe someone else's conversation was hooked into our line. I said, "Please, son, repeat that." Well, he said it again, the very same thing. Both my husband and I are in a daze. Is she trying to trap him? What should we tell our friends about the baby? Please help us.—*State Of Shock*

Dear State: If Everett is thirty-three, he's old enough to know what he's doing. Hope for the best, give them your blessings, and wish him luck. (He'll need it.) In the meantime, the fewer details to family and friends, the better.

Dear Ann Landers: I am twenty and have been married four years. My husband (who is twenty-six) has been having an affair with a sixteen-year-old girl. She used to sit with our children but I stopped calling her when I suspected something was going on. When I found some love letters from her in my husband's shirt pocket (she had mailed them to his office), I invited her to come over for a talk. She was very contrite (almost pathetic) and eager to do the right thing. She promised never to see my husband again. Well, she *is* seeing him, almost every night, and I don't know what to do. I can't get a straight sentence out of him. He is the world's biggest liar. Our religion allows only one marriage and this is it—lousy or not. The girl is underage, and I'd like to know if I can do anything legal to break this up.—*Cornsilk*

Dear Cornsilk: You can have your husband put in jail. But what would you have besides a husband in jail? The girl is the same age you were when you married the heel. If you'd like to write a letter for other sixteen-year-olds who think they are in love, I'd be happy to print it. For now, your best bet is to meet the competition with the type of ammunition you think would be most effective.

Dear Ann Landers: I am a fifteen-year-old girl who is awfully mixed up. The first problem is that I am a preacher's daughter and everybody expects me to be perfect. My parents are very strict. They keep reminding me that I have to live up to my station in life. I hate feeling that I am different from other girls my age, but that's the way it is, and I have accepted it. Two weeks ago a very nice boy walked me home from choir practice. Just before we reached our block he kissed me. I felt so guilty I couldn't sleep. A week later it happened again. Although I have prayed forgiveness, I feel I should tell my parents, but I can't bring myself to do it. I'm afraid I would be restricted for life. This morning I was so nervous I couldn't go to school. I told my mother I had a stomachache (which was true), but I'm sure my worries caused it. Can you help?—*Ashamed Of Myself*

Dear Ashamed: You need to have a long talk with your school counselor. I hope she tells you that kissing a boy is not a sin, and it is not necessary to report this to your parents. It is normal for a fifteen-year-old girl to want to be kissed by a boy. So long as the boy keeps his hands where they belong and you keep the situation under control, you need not feel guilty.

Dear Ann Landers: When I was fourteen, I made a big mistake with an older boy. Fortunately, I did not get pregnant. I read in your column recently where you said a girl should not tell her fiancé about such things. I hope you will not think I am dumb, but I would like to know if my fiancé will know about my mistake even if I don't tell him. I hope you dig what I am talking about.—*Sixteen But Not So Sweet*

Dear Not So: I dig, and the answer is probably not. Sometimes a girl who has never had sexual relations needs to undergo minor surgery, but this is rare. In most instances there is no 100 percent unmistakable evidence of virginity.

Dear Ann Landers: I am sixteen and very popular. In fact, too popular. Please believe me when I say I am still a good girl. I admit I have necked with several guys (I started to date when I was thirteen), but I have never done anything I am really ashamed of. The problem is that I get asked out so much and I like so many guys that sometimes I accept two dates in one evening. For example, I'll accept a date with Freddie from 7 till 10, and then I'll tell Teddie to come over at 10:15 and we'll go for a ride or a late show at the drive-in. It has come back to me that I am getting a pretty tacky reputation. I am only allowed to go out weekend nights and I have a 1:15 curfew, which I have never broken. Please tell me how I can improve my reputation.—*Angel Puss*

Dear Angel: The first thing you can do is cut out the second shift. A gal who has to stagger the traffic gives the impression that she is trying to break some sort of record. Although you obviously consider yourself virtuous because you are technically intact, I suspect you are crowding the line, which can be risky as well as damaging to a girl's reputation.

Dear Ann Landers: My wife suggested I write to you because our problem is one we don't want to discuss with anyone in this city. Last week our sixteen-year-old son came home from boarding school. He said he had something important to tell me. From the look on his face, I knew he was distressed. My first thought was, "He's gotten some girl in trouble." Well, Ann, I wish it were true. It would have been simple compared to the real problem. The boy confessed he is a homosexual. His mother and I are crushed. I blame myself for failing as a father. I feel guilty for not spending more time with him. My wife says this way of life was probably inflicted on him by the other boys at school. Is it possible? Our son has always been a fine student, an outstanding athlete, popular with both boys and girls. He is also very handsome, almost beautiful, which adds to the problem. Should we send him to a co-ed high school next fall? He says he doesn't want to see a doctor because he's not sick. I assure you that his mother and I *are*. Please advise.—*Heartbroken Dad*

Dear Dad: There's a chance that he might not be a homosexual. The amount of ignorance on this subject is appalling. A co-ed high school might be a good idea. A change of scenery and companions could be helpful. Be aware, however, that homosexuality cannot be inflicted on a normal male, so don't blame the school if it turns out that the boy *is* a homosexual. There is some disagreement among the experts regarding what causes homosexuality. While the vast majority of authorities agree it is the result of a poor child-parent relationship (often within the first four years of the youngster's life), there are other theories which should not be totally discounted. The important thing now is to get the boy to a psychiatrist and hope for the best. But don't expect magic. Experts report "cures" in less than 5 percent of the cases. Therapy can be extremely helpful, even if no "cure" occurs. It can help the boy accept himself as he is and adjust to his problem. Many homosexuals are creative and productive people and have made notable contributions to society.

Dear Ann Landers: Let me begin by saying I am a fourteen-year-old girl, and I don't know anything about the subject I am writing about. I mean venereal disease. I only know what I have read in magazines, and that's not much. Can a person get V.D. from kissing someone who has a sore on his lip? Could I get V.D. from kissing my aunt? How can a person tell if he has V.D. without going to a doctor? Where would a teen-ager go for treatment if he didn't want his parents to know? Please give me some information. I feel very ignorant and I can't talk to any adult about this. The kids in my crowd don't know any more than I do, and

they'd appreciate some information too.—*Curious An.
Needing Answers*

Dear Curious: First, it is possible to get V.D. from a
person (male or female) who has a sore on the lip, but
most people do not get it that way. The sore that
spreads V.D. is an active chancre, which means the
person with the sore has V.D. It is never a good idea
to kiss anyone who has an eruption of any kind. Even
if it isn't V.D., you don't need it, whatever it is. Self-
diagnosis is risky business. Anyone who suspects he
might be infected should see his family doctor at once.
He will in all probability treat you and not tell your
parents. If you have no family doctor, go to the city or
county health department. They will treat you free of
charge and not snitch if you ask them not to. (This is
the policy in Chicago and in most other cities.) And
while we are on the subject I would like to urge all
teen-agers to cooperate fully with the health officials
when they ask you to name your friends. This is not
rat-finking. It is your duty to tell the health officer
where you have been and with whom. The only way to
eradicate V.D. is to track down the sources of infection,
and everyone who can, should help.

Fourteen

WOULD YOU BELIEVE?

"Do you make up any of those letters?" is the question I am asked most often.

The answer is No, I do not. Every letter that appears in the Landers column, so far as I can determine, is strictly for real. No single mind would invent situations to compare with the true-to-life scenarios that cross my desk every day. To paraphrase Abraham Lincoln's famous line, "God must have loved the oddball—he made so many of them."

Any day's mail contains evidence that nothing is so ridiculous, so loony, so bizarre, but what somebody, somewhere won't do it. And why should this surprise us? Is there a single person who reads these words who has not had at least one experience that would read like a fabricated letter if it appeared in Ann Landers' column?

Occasionally the writer of an extraordinary letter will begin, "You're going to think I made this up, but so help me, every word is true." He then proceeds to unravel his fantastic story and I *do* believe him. How can I be sure the writer isn't putting me on? I can't be sure—completely sure—but through the years I've developed a sixth sense about phony letters.

I've learned to spot the clinkers much in the same way that a bank teller who handles money all day can spot a counterfeit. People in trouble don't write masterpieces. The far-out letter that is too well organized, too polished, too neat, is suspect. The genuine letter contains misspelled words, last-minute thoughts are scribbled in the margins, and sometimes the writer runs out of ink and finishes in pencil. The tone of humility and the sense of urgency would be impossible to fake.

Of course, I receive some phonies; everyone who writes for a newspaper does, but less than 3 percent of my mail falls into that category. The most literate phony letters come from New Haven, Connecticut. The Yale boys dearly love to fake me out. On occasion I have published a clinker from Yale and labeled it as such, but alas, these letters only serve to produce a blizzard of clinkers from Harvard boys who want to get into the act. Here's my favorite:

Dear Ann Landers: Please don't consider me crazy, but I need help and you are my only hope. My mother is bald, my father has a heavy head of hair. My older brother is losing his hair and will soon be bald like Mother. I am a circus acrobat. Hanging by my hair is part of my act. My hair is the same heavy type that Father has, but I become depressed worrying that perhaps my hair will fall out like Mother's. Should I change professions before it is too late?—*Clutched in Cambridge*

Dear Clutched: Don't be a coward. Even if you detect signs of baldness, stick with it. Bill yourself as the only balding acrobat who hangs by his hair. Don't chicken out and use a net. Good-bye and good luck.

Despite the letters which strain credulity and boggle the imagination, my column is an authentic reflection of life as it is lived by fifty million people. And since the kooks are a part of our society, is it not fitting and proper that their activities be represented in the daily chronicle of what's happening? So, in response to the question, "Would you believe?"—yes, I would.

———

Dear Readers: I printed a letter from an engaged girl who was making plans to be married. Her fiancé, she said, had a beautiful voice and wanted to sing a solo at their wedding. She asked if it would be proper. I told the girl that the groom is on hand to be married and not to entertain the guests, and in my opinion they had better get someone else to sing. Here is a sample of this week's mail:

Dear Ann Landers: Our daughter has been crying all day on account of you. Just last month we gave her a lovely wedding, and everyone said it was perfect down to the last detail. When Monica came down the aisle on her father's arm, her husband-to-be walked toward her singing "I Love You Truly." This added such a romantic touch to the ceremony that we received several letters about it from the guests. Now we see in your column that you feel it is in poor taste. Who appointed you judge and jury of the whole world?— *Short Hills, New Jersey.*

Dear Know-It-All Ann Landers: When my husband and I were married eighteen years ago, he took my arm from my father who had walked me down the aisle, we both faced the guests in the church, and he sang "Because." This was not planned; in fact it was a surprise to me, and I was thrilled. When our daughter is married, I hope her husband does the same thing. A spontaneous song from the groom is much more meaningful than a professional singer who gets paid.—*Burlington, Vermont*

Dear Ann Landers: You are so arrogant you make

me sick. Why do you feel that your way is the only way? I refer to your statement that it is in poor taste for a groom to sing at his own wedding. Our son married a lovely girl who had been married previously and was divorced. When the bride and groom met at the altar, she turned to him and sang "The Second Time Around." She is not a professional singer, Ann; in fact her voice is just fair, but everyone was so touched when she sang that song it was the talk of the town for weeks. You owe her an apology.—*Birmingham, Alabama*

Dear Ann Landers: I was very disappointed when you said it was in poor taste for the groom to sing at his own wedding. My fiancé and I are going to be married in April, and we have been rehearsing a duet. We had planned to sing "Each For The Other." At first Elwood was not very keen on the idea, but my mother and I talked him into it. Now, after what you said in your column, Elwood is getting balky again and if he refuses to sing it will be your fault. I wish you would mind your own business.—*Hutchinson, Kansas*

Dear Ann Landers: Our son is a fine organist. Eugene has played the organ at dozens of weddings, including his own. The ceremony was beautiful, and our son's exquisite music provided a fitting background. When the clergyman came to the portion of the service where Eugene's presence was required, he got up from the organ and all the guests applauded. Then he and his bride were married. Everyone said it was the most unusual wedding they had ever attended.—*Glendale*

After that barrage, I responded:

Dear Readers: Well, we have just heard from New Jersey, Vermont, Alabama, Kansas, and California—a good cross section of the country. It seems that people have been performing at their own weddings for quite some time, and there is every indication that they will continue to do so. If it makes the bride and groom happy and they are not concerned about the theatrical aspects, who am I to crab the act?

I felt sure my gracious retreat would close the subject, but I was wrong. Suddenly I was attacked from all sides by readers who were furious with me for reversing my stand. They wrote:

Hillsdale, Michigan: I was flabbergasted by the number of kooks who sang at their own weddings. If my husband had opened up his mouth to sing "I Love You Truly" when I walked down the aisle, I would have cracked up.

Long Island, New York: Where in the world were the clergymen when those balmy brides and goofy grooms sang during the wedding ceremony? Why did they permit the house of God to be used as a setting for a vaudeville act? If a couple is so happy they must give voice to their feelings, why can't they wait and sing at the reception?

Albuquerque, New Mexico: We of the Congregational Church do not permit sanctuary theatrics. Such exhibitionism has no place in a religious ceremony.

Chicago: I thank God every day for the canon law of the Presbyterian Church which makes it mandatory for the minister to approve all music to be played at weddings and funerals. Since I have occupied this pulpit I have had some outrageous requests. Recently I had to say No to a woman who wanted the church organist to play "Casey Jones" at her husband's funeral. "It was his favorite song," she sighed. "He would have wanted it that way."

Columbus, Ohio: No Roman Catholic ever sang at his own wedding. Our church does not tolerate such nonsense.

Davenport, Iowa: I feel very left out. I was married two years ago, and it was just an ordinary church wedding. My husband didn't burst out in song, my father-in-law didn't play the trombone, my little sister didn't do a toe dance, and my mother (who used to be a famous stripper) didn't go into her act. The guests must have been disappointed.

Houston: Here's a suggestion for those singing brides and grooms: Why not run an ad and sell tickets? The proceeds could help defray the honeymoon expenses—two weeks in the mental hospital of their choice.

Hutchinson, Kansas: Why were you surprised, Ann Landers, to discover that people sometimes sing at their own nuptials? That's pretty tame stuff. Every day a couple of screwballs get married on motorcycles, at home plate, on skates, atop a flagpole, on horseback, in jail, under water, and on a TV show to get free gifts. Recently I read where an English couple was married in the elevator where they first met. You, of all people, Ann, should know how crazy people can be.—*Mr. M.R.T.*

Dear M.R.T.: Amen, Brother. Amen. A reader sent this Associated Press item which appeared in the evening paper. Dateline: Corpus Christi: "A 19-year-old go-go dancer who does a topless act plans to marry between acts—still topless. Her maid of honor will also be topless. The justice of the peace who agreed to perform the ceremony said, 'I never question the dress of the people who ask to get married. My job is to get them married.'"

Dear Ann Landers: My great-uncle is eighty-four years old. Up until last year he was in very good health. Last week Uncle told us he plans to revise his will. We were shocked at what he wants in it. Uncle

insists on having a Viking funeral. I did not know what
a Viking funeral was until he explained it. The dead
person is put into a boat, the boat is set afire and
shoved out to sea. Uncle explained that this would not
be against the law, as the piece of property he owns
has a lake on it. The lake could be used instead of the
sea. I think this is a romantic way to go. The rest of
the family is appalled. Do you feel we should let Uncle
have his wish?—*Spokesman For The Relatives*

Dear Spokesman: I can't make this decision and neither can your relatives. Your state has burial laws, and
I know of no state which would permit a Viking funeral—even on a privately owned lake.

Dear Ann Landers: A year ago our two-year-old
son, Earl, had difficulty breathing so we took him to a
doctor. We learned Earl is allergic to cigarette smoke.
My husband said we both had to quit smoking right
then and there. He hasn't touched a cigarette since. I
went back to smoking that same night. I don't smoke
when little Earl is in the room, and it's awfully hard on
me. My husband doesn't know I smoke so I make excuses to go to the basement or out in the garage whenever I want a cigarette. Sneaking around is making me
nervous. Do you think it would be wrong if we let a
nice couple adopt Earl—a nice couple who doesn't
smoke? Then I could smoke in the open, and my husband could take it up again, too. The only problem is
that my husband is crazy about the boy. I love him,
too, but I am more the practical type. What do you
think, Ann?—*Mrs. E.R.M.*

Dear Mrs.: I think a lot of people who read this letter are going to say I made it up. It's incredible that a
mother would put cigarettes ahead of her own child.
Don't present this wild idea to your husband. I

wouldn't blame him if he decided to keep little Earl and unload *you.*

Dear Ann Landers: My mother-in-law doesn't like to write letters, She puts everything on postal cards, and I mean everything. Unfortunately, our mailman has a very big mouth. There is no such thing as a secret in this town.

A few weeks ago my mother-in-law wrote the following message on a card: "It's too bad the bank turned down your loan. I wish I could send you the money but I can't right now. If you would like me to speak to your Uncle Leonard, I will do so. You did pay back the money you borrowed from him to buy the car, didn't you?"

I boiled for weeks over that one. My husband said I was "sensitive."

This morning I received a card from her which said: "If you aren't having any success getting pregnant, Alice, why not talk to Martha? Maybe she will pass along some secret hints."

What do you think about this, Ann?—*Just Burning*

Dear Just: Personal business should not be written on postal cards, even if your mailman has a small mouth. Send your mother-in-law a box of self-addressed stamped envelopes with cards inside and tell her you'd appreciate it if she'd use them.

Dear Ann Landers: Our firm occupies an entire floor in one of the city's larger office buildings. The architect who planned this building must have hated females. The ladies' room is about half a block from our suite of offices, which employs thirty women. The men's room is directly across the hall.

I heard that a certain woman in the accounting department was seen going out of the men's room yesterday morning. I didn't believe it so I asked her. She said, "You bet it's true. I wouldn't think of hiking all the way down to the ladies' room." Any suggestions? —*Shocked Disbeliever*

Dear Shocked: Left alone, certain problems solve themselves. If that dame continues to use the men's room. something is bound to happen. Suddenly she'll decide it's worth the hike.

Dear Ann Landers: Perhaps if my children see this in your column they will believe it. I cannot seem to get through to them. Please ask your printers to put the next sentence in large type.

I DO NOT WANT A TV SET.

Let me explain. I am a widow with three lovely daughters. They are generous, kind, and thoughtful. Their husbands are grand, too. My children would do anything in the world for me.

For three years they have been trying to give me a TV set for Christmas, . Mother's Day, Easter—anything. I happen to enjoy the radio and I also read books. I don't want a TV set.

Yesterday my oldest daughter called and said, "Mother, please let us buy you a TV for Labor Day —even if you never turn it on. We want you to have one just so the neighbors can see the antenna."

I don't want a TV set, Ann, and I wish they'd quit pestering me. Please help.—*A Freak No Doubt*

Dear No Freak: Tell your children to skip the set and buy you an antenna.

Dear Ann Landers: I see by the wire services that a mortician in Georgia has gone in for drive-in display windows for those who want to view a deceased friend or relative but are too busy to park their cars and come inside. The mortician is constructing five windows six feet long—just the right size for an open coffin. The display will face a driveway at the side of the funeral home which is located on a busy street. The deceased will be lying in a lighted window, slightly tilted to make viewing easier. The mortician who dreamed up the idea says people seem to like it. According to him, folks are in a hurry these days and the drive-in display means they can come any hour of the day or night and they don't have to get dressed in their good clothes.—*Concerned*

Dear Concerned: The Russians have beat us again. Lenin has been on display under glass for years. "Have you seen the cold-cut yet?" is a question asked of American tourists who visit Moscow. In Russia, however, you must stand in line, sometimes for several hours. Digger O'Dell from Dixie seems to have come up with the ultimate in convenience. Or as they say in Georgia—"Man, that's really livin'."

Dear Ann Landers: I read recently that you are one of the ten most influential women in the United States. Since you have so much influence will you please see if you can send my husband on the first rocket to the moon? In the twenty-five years we have been married he has not been able to get along with a single person here on earth. Maybe he will find somebody up there that he can have a decent relationship with. Here are some of his pet theories: 1. Women marry men for one thing only—so they won't have to get up in the morning and go to work. 2. All politicians are crooks. 3. Income tax is unconstitutional because the government is spending money on a war that is undeclared. 4. People get warts from toads. 5. Psychiatry is a racket. What most kids need is a belt across the mouth, not analysis. Do you get the idea, Ann? I hope so. Please see what you can do about that spaceship to the moon. Thank you.—*Married To A Nut*

Dear Married: Sorry, I don't think they'd take him. He sounds too sick to travel.

Dear Ann Landers: I am in love with a twenty-one-year-old who has done something terrible. Last night Phil told me he was called up by the draft board and had to fill out a form. On the form he stated he was a homosexual. I asked why in the world he told such a lie and he replied, "Because I don't want to go into the Army, that's why." We talked for a long time and Phil said, "There are enough bums and loafers around who would rather go into the Army than work. I don't see why the government has to pull men away from good jobs when they don't want to go." If a man says he is a homosexual, is he excused from military service? If this is true, anyone who doesn't want to serve could use homosexuality as an excuse. Please tell me what the outcome will be.—*Outa My Skull*

Dear Skull: In most states, Phil would be called in for a psychiatric examination and asked for a letter of verification from his physician. Then he will be questioned by a psychiatrist who could determine from his answers that he is lying. Phil could be charged with fraud, which might mean time in the cooler, or he might be inducted promptly. The draft board will decide.

Dear Ann Landers: Are people crazier today than at any time in the history of man? I believe the answer is Yes. An item I just read in a newspaper is pretty good evidence. It seems a Mrs. P. Haverland of Charleston, West Virginia, has nothing better to do with her time than to try to break the record for being buried alive. The record is held by some flea-brain who lay in an underground casket for seventy-five days. Mrs. Haverland is sure she can set a new record. I would like to suggest that anyone who has seventy-five days to blow ought to go to some hospital and volunteer to break a record visiting the sick or writing letters for the disabled or just cheering up the lonely people in the nursing homes.—*Chicago Ruth*

Dear Chicago: People usually enjoy doing what they do best. Perhaps this is Mrs. Haverland's greatest talent.

Dear Ann Landers: Please, please, help a teen-age girl who is about to flip out. I had three dates this past weekend—one Friday night, one Saturday night, and a skating date Sunday afternoon. I need to know where a trend ends and nuttiness begins. I am talking about boys who are getting more girlish by the day. One boy asked to use my compact three times during the evening so he could comb his hair. He had a big wave in front and, I am not sure, but I think there were bobby pins holding it. My Saturday night date wore a jacket that was so fancy it looked like a girl's. I felt uncomfortable when he showed up in it, but I didn't say anything. The kid who took me out Sunday afternoon wore a shirt with a ruffled collar and cuffs. I thought it was his mother's. When I asked where he got it, he said it belonged to his brother. "I couldn't afford to get anything as nifty as this," he announced. The pants are getting tighter and the hair is getting longer and the clothes are getting fancier. Do boys want to be girls or what? Please tell me. I am beginning to wonder what all this means.—*Miss?????*

Dear Miss: Marshall McLuhan says clothes these days are not clothes but costumes. People are dressing for the roles they play. I believe he has a message. The more bizarre the outfit, the more desperate the "actor."

Well-balanced individuals are not compelled to do everything short of set their hair on fire to attract attention. And for those who have already reached for their ballpoints to tell this square old lady what's "in," save your stamps. I *know* what's in, and I wouldn't wear some of the so-called in styles to a skunk rassle.

Dear Ann Landers: I had to laugh at the letter from the person who said he thought you made up the stuff that appeared in the newspaper because people couldn't be that loony. I, for one, can tell you he is mistaken. A situation exists right under my nose that nobody would believe if you printed it. Some friends of ours (two couples) love to dance. They started to go out to public dances together. Suddenly they discovered each one danced better with the other one's mate. So they switched. Right now they are just a happy bunch of nuts, getting ready to divorce each other so they can change partners for life: And get a load of this—they are looking to buy one big house so they can live together. Nobody is mad at anybody; it's just as cozy as it can be. Print this as proof that people are wacky.—*Veritas*

Dear Veritas: Who needs proof?

A letter about Kelly, a dog who wouldn't eat meat on Friday, unloosed a torrent of testimonials which strongly suggest that our furred and feathered friends are at least as smart as people—if not smarter. Here are some samples from my mail:

From Highland Park: If you think Kelly's dog is unusual, what would you say about our English setter, Leviticus? We got Lev when he was four months old —a gift from friends who are deeply religious. These friends adhere to the dietary laws of their faith. Leviticus not only refuses to eat meat which is not kosher but the meat must be served to him on a Yiddish newspaper. We have tried the Chicago *Sun-Times* and the *Daily News,* but Lev cannot be foooled.—*Right Hand Up*

Dear Right Hand Up: I have no comment whatever to make on Leviticus. Particularly since Mrs. Helen Palmer, the women's editor of the Toronto *Star,* sent me a clipping from that paper describing a kosher cat, owned by Rabbi Louis Farrell. The mixing of meat and milk is forbidden by Orthodox Jewish law. Rabbi Farrell's cat must have known this because he refused to drink milk when meat was served. Frequently the kosher cat demonstrated his dedication to this dietary law for guests—to their utter amazement.

From Miami: I don't want to take anything away from Kelly's dog, but did you know there was a chimpanzee down in Daytona Beach who used to play gin rummy? His master began by letting the chimp play a few hands for kicks. When that chimp blitzed one of the best card players in Florida in three hands, the boys got mad and wouldn't let the monkey sit in the game.

From Seattle: Our Weimaraner, Ellsworth, loves classical music. He sits meditatively when Ormandy or Bernstein recordings are on the hi-fi. When the kids put on rock 'n' roll, Ellsworth leaves the room. Several months ago our daughter bought some Beatles records. Ellsworth whined and moaned and finally put his paw on the knob and turned the machine off.

From Columbus, Ohio: Our dog Strib was only a mutt, but he was an awfully smart mutt. When I was four years old, Mom announced to the family that we were going to have a new baby in the house. The very next morning Strib went out for his morning walk and returned carrying a baby shoe in his mouth. He proudly laid it at Mother's feet. For the next several months he kept bringing home baby shoes—about one every two weeks. This went on until the new baby came. Then he stopped.

From Kansas City: Our oldest daughter went with a guy I never could warm up to. When he came to call, our beagle had to be put in the back hall. Sparky hated that fellow and he sure did show it. She married the guy and he turned out to be a rat. I told my two younger daughters I didn't want any fellows coming to the house a second time if Sparky didn't like 'em. This may sound nutty, but both girls used Sparky as a guide, and today they are married to two fine young men and are very happy.

From California: Our myna bird, Socrates, had a fairly large vocabulary and did a good bit of talking. We always thought myna birds were strictly imitators. Now I'm not sure. Three days before the California election for governor, I was having an argument with a friend. I said to him, "I'll bet you twenty dollars Pierre Salinger will win!" Socrates poked his head through the cage and shrieked, "No, no, Murphy will win!" Murphy did win. How do you like them apples?— *Santa Barbara*

Dear Santa: I bet on Salinger, so you *know* how I liked them apples!

Dear Ann Landers: I have been engaged to Burt for so many years I'm ashamed to tell you the number. We were supposed to get married three months ago. I had my dress bought and my hair fixed. Then his horse got sick. I am still single. Burt spends every spare minute at the barn. He has broken dozens of dates with me because his horse didn't look right He'd rather sit around with the vet and worry about the horse than be with me. I like horses, but I like people better. I am beginning to think Burt is different. He eats, dreams, and thinks horses. He even smells like a horse most of the time. Any advice?—*Disgusted*

Dear Disgusted: It appears you have been left at the post, dearie. If you are running so poorly before marriage, I'd say your chances for getting any attention whatever after marriage are about 100 to 1—against. As for Burt, I suggest he take a saliva test.

Dear Ann Landers: You can print this letter just as I am writing it because everyone in town already knows about it anyway. Our neighbors have a parrot named Plato. This parrot is so smart it is frightening. When Plato rattles off radio and TV commercials he sounds just like the announcers. His Edward P. Morgan imitation is the greatest. The other evening our neighbors had a party. The guests gathered to listen to Plato do his routine. Suddenly Plato shrieked, "Bernie cheats on his wife. Bernie cheats on his wife" Bernie is my husband, and I didn't think it was funny. All the guests roared. Do parrots know what they are saying or do they just pick up phrases and repeat them? I've heard a variety of opinions, and I'd appreciate an answer from you.—*Standing By*

Dear Standing By: Parrots do *not* know what they are saying. They imitate sounds. I suspect this is a well-rehearsed gag, and if I were you, I'd forget about it.

Dear Ann Landers: Ever since you printed that letter from the woman who has a parrot that imitates voices on the radio (especially mine), I've been getting letters asking, "Will the real Edward P. Morgan please stand up?" I don't want a cracker, Ann. I want help. The sponsors of my program are disturbed. They want to know if the parrot is a member of the Actor's

Union. I am disturbed, too, because if she is, they might decide to replace me. The parrot probably would work cheaper and be more of a novelty. An aunt of mine, looking for a possible legacy from the J. P. Morgan family, once traced our family tree. She found no connection with the financier but learned that we are direct descendants from Henry the Pirate. It is possible that Henry mistreated his parrot and this bird who imitates me has inherited the resentment. Do you have any solace handy?—*Edward P. Morgan*

Dear Ed: We just checked with the parrot and you can relax. She is not after your job. She says the reason parrots live for two hundred years is that they are too smart to get mixed up with tension-producing jobs on radio, TV—or newspapers.

Dear Ann Landers: We have two sons. For almost three years my husband and I have wanted another child but we've had no luck. About a month ago my sister said she'd like to try the needle trick on me to determine whether or not I'd have more children. She took a threaded needle and rubbed it across my middle finger. Then she dangled the threaded needle over the top of my hand, steadying it between her thumb and index finger until it stood perfectly still. If the needle remained still it meant that I would not have any more children. If it moved back and forth it meant a boy. If it moved in circles it meant a girl. We tried it three times. Twice the needle moved back and forth, meaning I had two boys, which was right. The third time it stood still, indicating I would not have any more children. This past week six different women tried it on me, and the results were the same every time. I know this sounds nutty, but the accuracy of these tests is amazing. How do you explain it?—*D.L.*

Dear D.L.: I won't try. But this I can tell you—if

you really want another child, put your faith in the
needle trick. Give away your baby buggy, your crib,
the stroller, and the diaper pail. Accept the fact that
you will never have more children. Chances are excellent that within a year you'll be pregnant. The fre-
quency with which this has occurred is more amazing
than the needle trick.

Dear Ann Landers: This may not happen to me
again in a million years, and if it does, that will be
soon enough. But I need to know what to do, just in
case. My boyfriend Robbie and I have had eleven
dates, not counting the time he has come over just to
talk. Last night was the night I have been dreaming
about for six months. He kissed me good night. It
turned out to be more like a nightmare than a dream.
Robbie wears braces and so do I. Somehow our braces
got hooked together, and it was the most embarrassing
thing that has happened to me in my whole life. We
were hooked for only a few seconds, but it seemed like
an eternity before I was able to jiggle my head and dis-
connect us. He was embarrassed, too, but he didn't say
anything. I'm afraid Robbie may never want to kiss me
again. What can I do to make sure this doesn't happen
anymore?—*Tomato Face*

Dear Tomato: Ask your dentist to check for loose
or hookable wires on your braces and suggest that
Robbie do the same. And P.S.: It just might be that
you two kids are putting too much heart and soul into
that good-night kiss. Cool it.

Dear Ann Landers: My husband started having life-
like dreams about six weeks ago. Arnold woke up exhausted, said he dreamed he had swum the English
Channel with Johnny Weissmuller. He couldn't go to
work until noon. A few weeks later he woke up in a

cold sweat. He said he had dreamed he was a captain under General Custer and the Indians had given him a very rough time. Arnold had the shakes so bad at breakfast that I called the doctor. He sent over some tranquilizing pills. This morning my husband woke up in great pain. He had dreamed he broke his leg scuba-diving. He limped around all day and couldn't get his shoe on, so he didn't go to work. Ten times I said to him, "Look, Arnold, you know it was a dream, don't you? So if it didn't actually happen, how come your leg hurts?" He replied. "Your guess is as good as mine." Please tell me what to do.—*Mrs. L.J.G.*

Dear Mrs. L.J.G.: Since your husband is so good at dreaming, it's too bad he doesn't treat himself to something better than a fight with Indians or a broken leg. If Arnold's dreams persist he should talk to his physician. When fantasy and reality get so close together, help may be needed.

Dear Ann Landers: Many years ago I attended a convention where the ladies all seemed to be wearing silk dresses with floral patterns and big hats. My aunt was being installed as president. This was back in the days when falsies were inflatable, like balloons. Well, the outgoing president made a gushy speech and closed with: "It is an honor for me to present you with this corsage as a token of our esteem and affection." She then proceeded to pin the corsage on Auntie. *Bang!* went the balloon, and half of her dimensions changed right there in front of two thousand people. Naturally this was the highlight of the convention. People still laugh about it fifteen years later.—*No Town for Gosh Sakes*

Dear No Town: If you ever hear of a contest for the most embarrassing moment, Auntie has the first prize in her pocket. (And I hope it's not a medal!)

Dear Ann Landers: Several weeks ago my boyfriend Dale asked if he could dress up in my clothes just for the fun of it. I thought he was joking, but when he showed me the wig he had bought for himself I knew he was serious. When Dale dressed up and put on makeup, he looked like a very pretty girl. I couldn't get over it. He said it would be a great gag to take a walk and see if any fellows made passes at us. I was curious to find out if he could get away with it so I agreed. I know this sounds crazy, Ann, but Dale got more whistles than I did—and he loved it. He is not a homosexual. We have a very good sex life. He is normal in every way. This business of dressing like a girl is just for kicks. I'd like to marry Dale but this small detail bothers me. Please set my mind at ease.—*Rosie*

Dear Rosie: Dale is a transvestite. This does not mean he's a homosexual, but it is a deviation, nonetheless. If you want to marry a man who enjoys wearing your clothes and getting passes from men, go ahead. Normal it isn't, lady.

Dear Ann Landers: I was deeply disappointed in your answer to the woman whose boyfriend enjoyed dressing up in her clothes. You didn't come right out and say the man was a weirdo, but you made it obvious that you considered him mighty odd. My wife and I are happily married, and we have three lovely children. I have been wearing my wife's girdle for several years, and I am not ashamed of it. I wear a girdle because it makes my back feel better and it improves my posture. I also wear nylons under my wool socks because I need something to hold my girdle down. I trust you will print this letter in the interest of fairness. I always thought you were open-minded.—*Dallas Golfer*

Dear Dallas: I try to be open-minded, but that doesn't mean I have holes in my head. I was all set to go along with your girdle, for health reasons, although a surgical corset designed for males with back problems would have made more sense. But when I read that bit about the nylons, you lost *my* support completely. A word of advice to you, Old Buddy: Don't let the guys in the locker room get a load of your undies or you're going to have a lot more trouble than you need.

I thought my response to the Dallas Golfer would button it all up, but I was wrong. Within the week I received an avalanche of letters from virtually every state in the union. Here are some samples:

Dear Ann Landers: Why do you point an accusing finger at any man who happens to prefer some article of women's clothing? Some men enjoy a soft, smooth fabric next to their skin. Somewhere along the line men got stuck with cotton underwear. I can assure you if men's silk shorts were not so expensive, they would outsell cotton shorts by the carload. Shortly after I married, my wife was making a dress for herself. We are both the same height. She asked me to put on her dress so she could pin the hem properly. I liked the feel of the silk dress and asked her if she would make one for me to lounge in. Now I have several lounging dresses, and they are much more comfortable than slacks and a T-shirt. I'm not a fairy and I resent the inference that any man who wears women's clothes is a little funny.—*Dyersville, Iowa*

Dear Dy: My haberdashery expert tells me cotton shorts are plenty soft enough for anybody and that most men prefer cotton shorts to the sleazier fabrics. I would not try to change the mind of a guy who sits around in his wife's dresses, however, so enjoy yourself, Bub.

Dear Ann Landers: I would like to comment on the letters from those men (?) who are lounging around in their wives' dresses, wearing bloomers, nylons, and high heels, and yet they have the nerve to say they do it for kicks and that they are perfectly normal. Many of those nuts said they were married and have children. So what? Marriage and children are not proof of normalcy. Queers often marry to gain respectability and put up a smoke screen. Men who get their kicks dressing up in women's clothes are not normal, and it baffles me how a smart woman like you can be taken in by such rubbish? Don't you know they are homosexuals? If you don't know it you have no business being a human relations counselor. I hope you will set the record straight once and for all.—*No Curlycues*

Dear Curly: I didn't say they were normal. *They* said they were normal. I am well aware that something is off-kilter when a man gets a charge out of wearing his wife's underwear. And since you want to keep the record straight, you are wrong when you make the flat statement that these men are homosexuals. Most of them are not. They are most likely transvestites. Any good unabridged dictionary explains the difference.

Dear Ann Landers: Many men enjoy dressing up in women's clothing. I, for one, can tell you it's a real kick in the head. Here's how I discovered how much fun it could be. Several years ago my wife and I went to a "Switch Sex Ball" at our country club. My wife wore our oldest son's suit. I wore one of her made-over evening dresses, her wig and white fox stole. My wife did my makeup (false eyelashes and the works), and she even painted my fingernails. I won first prize as the "Fooler Female." I enjoyed the outfit so much I decided to wear it again several nights later when the two of us took a weekend vacation. We posed as two women friends and no one batted an eye. Now I have several "fooler" outfits, and whenever we are out of town we enjoy a few evenings out as "women." This may seem strange, but I assure you I am perfectly normal. These little masquerade parties are simply our way of having fun.—*All Man*

Dear Man: Yup. You're all normal—all you guys who like to dress up in women's clothes. And if anyone says otherwise, just hit 'em with your purse, dearie.

ABOUT THE AUTHOR

As the wife of Jules Lederer, President of Budget Rent-A-Car, ANN LANDERS spends ten to twelve hours a day personally answering each of the thousands of letters she receives from all over the world. Thirteen years ago she began writing the Ann Landers column for the Chicago SUN-TIMES. Today her syndicated column appears in more than 700 newspapers around the world with a readership of 54 million.

Miss Landers is the author of two best-selling books, *Since You Ask Me* and *Ann Landers Talks to Teen-Agers About Sex.*

BANTAM BESTSELLERS

OUTSTANDING BOOKS NOW AVAILABLE
AT A FRACTION
OF THEIR ORIGINAL COST!

SOUP'S ON!

AMERICA'S FAVORITE RECIPES FROM BETTER HOMES & GARDENS. From appetizers to luscious desserts —over 500 prize-tested recipes—275 photographs!
(NE4578—95¢)

HAWAII COOKBOOK & BACKYARD LUAU by Elizabeth Ahn Toupin. 175 succulent recipes plus tempting menu suggestions to turn your kitchen into an exotic tropical paradise
(SE13—75¢)

James Beard's HORS D'OEUVRES & CANAPES. Great for party-giving success—sizzling taste treats and cool bite-size delights.
(SE4384—75¢)

THE ART OF BARBECUE COOKING. What to cook on— what to cook with—full-color photographs of many appetizing dishes—plus a special chapter on sauces. (NE4782—95¢)

THE FANNIE FARMER JUNIOR COOKBOOK by Wilma Lord Perkins. The famous, illustrated guide that's been the favorite of young cooks for over two decades. (SE4677—75¢)

THE COMPLETE BOOK OF MEXICAN COOKING by Elisabeth Ortiz. 340 delicious recipes in the most complete and colorful guide to Mexican cooking ever written.
(NE4107—95¢)

THE SPANISH COOKBOOK by Barbara Norman. Precise and simple directions for over 200 of the best recipes from the kitchens of Spain.
(SE4389—75¢)

AN HERB AND SPICE COOKBOOK by Craig Clairborne. The food editor of *The New York Times* presents over 400 original and tempting recipes, prepared with dozens of different herbs and spices—a subtle choice of the finest cuisine throughout the world.
(NE5427—95¢)

Ask for them at your local bookseller or use this handy coupon:

Wait 'til you see what *else* we've got in store for you!

Send for your FREE catalog of Bantam Bestsellers today!

This money-saving catalog lists hundreds of bestsellers originally priced from $3.75 to $15.00—yours now in Bantam paperback editions for just 50¢ to $1.95! Here is a great opportunity to read the good books you've missed and add to your private library at huge savings! The catalog is FREE! So don't delay—send for yours today!